This is a great book. It was easy to read and stuffed full of practical suggestions on how to organise myself and my teams to get things done. Over the years I have read lots of these types of books and this is one of the best because it felt like it was really focused on helping me achieve the things I wanted to achieve.

Simon Carter, head of media relations for the Scout Association

Steve has done it again with a book that draws on his inspiring and unique journey through setting a vision and path to get to his own GOLD and helps us to do the same step by step. Steve's incredible journey reminds us that our GOLD is worth working for and the exercises in this book empower you to do just that.

Charlene Friend, CFO, Focus Group

Many books are inspiring, but Steve combines the inspiration of his own story with practical takeaways to leave the reader feeling both motivated and equipped for their journey. An excellent and engaging read.

Professor Paul McGee, aka The Sumo Guy, *Sunday Times* bestselling author

In this book, Steve brings to life how he analysed and made sense of his sporting achievements. By breaking down the process using simple exercises and simplifying some complex theoretical concepts, he makes the process very accessible. What I really like is that the book is both a standalone aid, but also part of a whole toolkit developed to help any individual achieve their GOLD using the approach that suits their learning style. It is easy, reading this, to see why Steve has achieved so much both in sport and in his chosen business career.

Zahara Hyde OBE, CEO, British Triathlon 2008–2014

Steve's book GOLD really inspires you, the reader to think passionately about what you really want to achieve in life. His scouting background along with the personal stories combined with the suggested tasks throughout the book motivate and empower you to take immediate action on your journey. A compelling and uplifting read.

Tim Kidd OBE, former UK chief commissioner for the Scout Association

Why settle for silver when Steve Judge will show you the winning ways to GOLD?

Michael Heppell, Internationally acclaimed speaker and bestselling author

GOLD

5 **winning ways**
to unlock the power of your
potential and achieve your goals

STEVE JUDGE

World champion athlete and global speaker

Gold
ISBN 978-1-912300-84-6
eISBN 978-1-912300-85-3

Published in 2023 by Right Book Press
Printed in the UK

© Steve Judge 2023

Contents

Foreword

At 8.04 pm on 17 September 2022, something amazing happened to me.

It was at that exact moment that I crossed the finishing line of Ironman Maryland, 13 hours, 4 minutes and 53 seconds after I started. This realised a goal I'd had since I entered my first 5k running event some 15 years previously. An Ironman is the ultimate triathlon – a 2.4-mile swim, a 112-mile bike ride, and a 26.2-mile run. That's right, it finishes with a marathon.

Now don't worry. If that's making you feel tired already, you don't have to compete in an Ironman. That was my goal, or as Steve says – my GOLD. Your GOLD will be whatever it is for you – be that an endurance sporting event, a target in your business or something personal you're working towards.

Steve's GOLD process might have not been documented in this book when I was training for and completing the Ironman, but the parallels between the process I underwent and GOLD are uncanny. Put simply, his process works.

Steve's incredible story and the steps he has taken to become the success he is are, and you'll have to pardon the pun, *gold*. When he talks about visualising your success, even to the extent of drawing your future self, it is powerful stuff. As I read it, and then saw his picture of his intended future success, it was one of those moments that made the hair stand up on the back of my neck.

As national director for BNI in the UK & Ireland, I was responsible for setting the vision and the goals for the organisation. I encouraged the franchisee team, the support teams, the office team and of course BNI members to go for their GOLD. But being a leader of an organisation can be a lonely place. I would have given anything to be able to inspire my teams and get the hair standing up on the back of their necks!

I've seen Steve speak on the stage – he is a wonderful performer with a compelling story that inspires you to take action. This book is just the same, and I would highly recommend you look into his workshops (both elearning and in person) as an accompaniment.

I'm at a stage in my life where I'm embarking on a new direction. Having sold my BNI business last year, I've set up a new business, Unnatural Success Ltd, helping introverts within the professional services industry to be confident to generate business through networking.

The beauty of how Steve has put this book together is it's not just a book. He encourages you to take action straight away – so you do. Guess what – I've been following along, and as I write this, I've just spent the period between Christmas and New Year visualising, planning and setting my GOLD for my new business.

Now I'm at this new stage of my life, with a new business to bring to market and new goals to achieve, *GOLD* might as well have been written for me personally! I think you'll find that it feels like Steve has written *GOLD* for you personally too.

Now... how about the next Ironman? 13 hours, 4 minutes and 53 seconds is beatable, right?

Charlie Lawson
Former national director, BNI UK & Ireland

Hell on earth is...

'Do you know what hell on earth is?' asked my business coach, Rob Pickering, during one of our sessions. 'Hell on earth,' he continued, 'is getting to the end of your days and meeting the person that you could have become.'

I sat for a while as I absorbed this quote and the meaning behind it. I went through it again and again in puzzlement. So how do *you* understand this quote? If you accept it, you're saying that at the end of your days, you will see yourself lying in your hospital bed, thinking of all the things that you didn't do and all those missed opportunities that you let fly by. And to make things even worse, the person you meet will be your alter ego – the high-flying, successful and happy self who grabbed every opportunity that came their way and lived their life with no regrets.

Or do you reject it?

The way I see it is that, at the end of my days, I know I will have reached my full potential. In health, fitness and work, I will have grabbed every opportunity and lived my life with no regrets, ensuring that I will have become a successful, high achiever in my own right. The person I could have been will be the loser. For that reason, I reject it – I reject the quote.

Meeting the person that I could've been, at the end of my days, would not be hell on earth; in fact, I would take satisfaction from seeing the negative person that I could have become. I'd give them a pat on the back for all the hard work and effort that made my life as fulfilling as possible. This concept fuels me to keep going in my endeavours and carry on working hard towards my goals – to keep grabbing those opportunities that are presented to me, to follow my heart and do the things I love and to embrace my desires and the dreams that will bring me happiness.

'I don't get it,' I said to Rob. 'I don't understand why meeting the person I could have become is a negative.' He smiled at me and said, 'No, Steve, I didn't think you would but most people who read that quote do think it's a negative – around 80 per cent.' Those few words blew my mind and opened up my perception of how a person's mindset can greatly affect what they believe and consequently what they can achieve.

There's something inside me that gets agitated by this. It feels as if somebody's rattling the cage of the white tiger inside me. My inner tiger wants to burst out and do something. It wants to growl and roar (do tigers roar or is that just lions?). Either way I feel energised to do something, anything, to help people realise that in life you only get one chance. I know this and can speak from experience because of what I've been through. I've found out that you really must grab this thing called life with both hands and do something with it every day, every week, month and year.

I love this quote attributed to Confucius: 'We have two lives and the second begins when we realise we only have one.' I get it because I had an epiphany, a second chance, a new beginning. This realisation came from the near-fatal car accident that I endured and the traumatic experiences that it dragged me through. This book is about what I did following the accident and the journey that took me from wheelchair to world champion and beyond. By sharing my experiences, my knowledge and my learnings, I want people to be empowered, inspired and motivated by my story so that they can go forward on their own journey in the direction of fulfilment. I hope that by doing this, the pain and suffering I have endured will not have been in vain.

I believe that how people interpret the 'hell on earth' quote is the key to how they run their life and ultimately whether or not they live with no regrets. I started wondering how many people this might affect – how many focus on the future and achieve what they want and how many dwell on their avoidance and consequently don't achieve what they want.

Rob had the answer. 'It's the 80–20 rule,' he said. I was aware of the 80–20 rule from my engineering days. Some call it the Pareto principle. The 80–20 rule started off as an observation of results and statistics by the engineer and economist Vilfredo Pareto back in 1906, stating that 80 per cent of consequences come from 20 per cent of the causes. Although it is not a law of nature it's uncanny how many studies and figures seem to align themselves with this ratio.

So what Rob was implying was that 80 per cent of people are motivated by moving away from the negative stuff, while only 20 per cent are motivated purely by moving towards the good stuff. Ask people why they work: more will say 'To pay the bills or else I'll lose my house' and fewer will say 'To buy a bigger house' or similar. The way I interpreted this was that 80 per cent of people concentrate on the things that they don't want and only 20 per cent focus on what they do want and actively work towards it. I found this baffling.

GOLDEN NUGGET

'Where focus goes, energy flows.'
– Tony Robbins (Twitter, May 2020)

That means most people repeatedly say to themselves things like 'I don't want to be overweight' rather than saying

'I want to be slim and fit.' Or, 'I don't like this job' rather than 'I want to be in a place where I love to work.'

But then I wondered, 'So what?' What difference does it make if you focus on achievement or on avoidance? Does this really make a difference to your achievements? Can this be the source of becoming a high achiever in all that you do? Is there a correlation between high achievers and how they focus on their goals?

High achievers constantly focus on what they want to achieve. They focus on working towards success and the accolades that they will accumulate on their journey. This confirms the theory that if you want to be a high achiever, the most important thing to do is to focus on what you want to achieve rather than what you want to avoid.

- 'I will be fit and healthy.'
- 'I will help and empower people.'
- 'I will be happy and content in life.'

There may not seem to be a massive difference between one approach or the other but if people are not focusing on something that they want to achieve then they are not encouraging themselves to move forward. They are probably not making plans or setting life goals.

GOLDEN NUGGET

'Life is neither easy nor hard. Life is a journey in which we face challenges that help bring out the best version of ourselves.'
– Rob Pickering

An equally important question is whether or not the people who struggle to achieve can ultimately become high achievers. I believe the answer to this is 'yes'. With the right amount of awareness, guidance and coaching, I believe that people can fulfil their dreams. This is part of my vision and my goal and therefore why I've written this book. It's also why I share my keynote speeches and run my workshops.

So, I guess the important question is this: which kind of person are you? Going back to the original quote, would meeting the person that you could have become be a good thing or a bad thing? Do you dream of succeeding rather than avoiding failure? On your journey, are you willing to push yourself out of your comfort zone through the challenging mountains of insecurity rather than 'flatlining' through the valley of life? If you don't go after what you want then you'll never have it. If you don't ask, you don't get and if you don't take a step forward then you'll always end up in the same place. Are you being the best that you can be every day? Are you living your life with no regrets?

Happy and content?

Because of what happened to me and my realisation about how precious life is, I now want to make the most of it. I'm always thinking of what else I can do so that at the end of the day, week, month or even at the end of my life, I can look back and say to myself, 'No regrets.' For example, I'm extremely happy in my life. I have a loving partner, my two kids are awesome and I'm fit and well. I love my job and literally wake up every morning motivated to push forward in my business – and it's even better when I'm performing on stage. I'm always smiling but I'd also say that I'm not necessarily content. I have so much more that I want to give, do and achieve and that's what I'm working towards. To be honest, I'm also impatient about it and that drives me forward as I unleash my white tiger from within, using its power, strength, ferocity and energy to take control and make things happen.

I've written this book specifically for people who want to be the best that they can be every day and take them on a journey from where they are to where they want to be, both personally and professionally. This book will help those who feel that they are stuck or want change or who feel that something is missing in their life. It's for those who want to grab life with both hands and live it with no regrets. It's for those who are not content or even happy with where they are right now and those who want success and to become high achievers.

This book will also enhance teams by empowering each team member to move forward on their journey. As individuals move forward while supporting each other, they will build the overall incentive and success of the team. In many situations it's about the team and how personal achievements come together towards one big organisational goal. That's the key. It's not just about you; it's about who surrounds you. It's about your 'golden gang' — which I'll cover later.

I believe that everybody deserves the right to experience the happiness and fulfilment of achieving their true life goals. This book will empower you and your team and inspire and motivate all who travel on the journey in the direction of their vision — the GOLD in their life.

The meaning of your GOLD

Your GOLD is your burning desire within that ignites the passion, dedication and commitment required to achieve.

- G stands for your **goal** – the specific target you have focused on that you get excited about working towards and gets you jumping out of bed in the morning.
- O stands for your **opportunity** – when you see it, hear it or even smell it, you're going to grab it with both hands and take action to achieve and succeed.
- L is your **love** – what or who do you love? What is that thing or who is that person that brings you ultimate joy and happiness and ignites that warm glow inside?
- D stands for your **dream** or even your **desire** – when you close your eyes and imagine euphoria, what is the image, where do you go? Where are you, what are you doing, who are you with?

GOLDEN NUGGET

'True passion attracts. If you have passion in your business, the right people will be attracted to your team.'
– Robert Kiyosaki

But it's not just about knowing what your GOLD is, it's about knowing everybody else's, especially if they are on your team. Knowing what each other's focus and desires are helps everybody to work together and move in the same direction towards success. This book will take you, your team, your department and your business on a journey to discover your GOLD.

GOLDEN NUGGET

'Action is the foundational key to all success.'
– Pablo Picasso

The golden key

To unlock the power of your potential and achieve your GOLD you will need a key, a golden key. This key represents the action that is needed because, after all, this is the only thing that creates change. Taking action step by step on your journey will move you ever closer to achievement. By completing the exercises throughout the chapters of this book you will be taken in the right direction towards your GOLD for it to be unlocked.

The golden compass

I've discovered what it takes to find what you really want and, most importantly, how to achieve it. I've discovered that achieving your GOLD comes down to five strategies that form a compass. This has given me direction as I travel towards my GOLD – a golden compass, if you will.

In this book, I will share each strategy to help you find and achieve your greatest desire. The stories that I'll share from my rehabilitation, my life as an athlete and my work as a speaker will detail how and what I have achieved throughout my journey, taking me from wheelchair to world champion and beyond.

Chapter 2 will help you prepare for your journey towards your GOLD by giving you the tools to find out where you are now and in which direction you want or need to go. Then Chapters 3 to 7 will cover the five strategies that are transforming the lives of people around the world and empowering them to visualise their ultimate desire and then go forth to achieve it.

Your golden vision

Finding your vision – your GOLD – as a focus for your energy is crucial to the success of the journey and one of the most important attributes of high achievers. Learning the desires of each individual member of a team will promote its overall success.

Your golden soul

When the going gets tough your 'golden soul' will keep you going. Knowing the true purpose of your mission empowers you to continue when you may feel like quitting. Sharing your reasons reminds others around you why you started and fuels the passionate fire inside you.

Your golden gear

Discovering what 'golden gear' you need to accomplish your journey will set you off on the right foot. Knowing the tools of your trade will take you to the highest peak of your potential and will enable you and your team to succeed.

Your golden gang

You can't do this journey alone and your 'golden gang' will support, mentor and teach you as you go forward on your journey. Not just in the commencement and achievement stage but also looking forward to fulfilment. The golden gang members that you haven't even yet met are the ones who will take you to an even higher plane.

Your golden hour

Every hour, day, week, month and year will take you forward, step by step, towards your overall GOLD. This strategy will help you see and coordinate the complete timeline towards your future self. It will show you how the most extraordinary life is waiting for you and how you can take it one 'golden hour' at a time.

Your golden guidebook

As you work your way through this book, it will guide you towards an understanding of each strategy and carrying out the exercises will give you practical solutions on your journey towards conceiving, believing and achieving your GOLD. But before I go into the five strategies, I'll explain who I am and what I've been through. I found out that we can't always control what happens to us but we can control how we react to what happens to us. So, when my life took a U-turn, instead of saying 'Why me?' I learned to say 'Try me!'

This book complements my Good to GOLD workshop. For more details and for free downloads to accompany your journey to GOLD, go to **steve-judge.co.uk/good-to-gold-resources-page**

Chapter 1
My golden journey

From coal to GOLD

Sunday 26 April 2002

Life was great and all going to plan – if there is such a thing as a plan, that is. But driving home from a friend's house that Sunday afternoon, I could never have imagined how my life was about to turn upside down. I was 28 years old and getting married to my fiancée in three months' time. The stag do was imminent and the wedding plans were all sorted. I had a good job as a quality manager at a firm based in Doncaster which had great prospects for promotion and development. This was not my first job since leaving school because at 16 I was working down the coal pits of Yorkshire. The job had been OK but I wasn't content so I took myself off to college, studied and trained to become a mechanical engineer and specifically a maintenance fitter. I don't know what the hell those guys did to those machines down the pit but when they broke down, it was my job to go down and fix them. I couldn't lean on any excuses. Those machines needed to be fixed and at times I had to be ingenious in the things that I did to get them working again. In my job, I was constantly presented with problems, and I had to find solutions.

I was fit and well – in fact I was very fit as I loved the outdoor life and always had. I was heavily involved in Scouting and had always loved gaining the badges for my uniform. Looking back, working towards them laid the foundation for setting goals and moving towards them. The first three badges I ever received happened to be swimming, cycling and running, which became significant in my later years.

I loved running as a kid and I'd do it with the rest of my family – my mum, dad, brother and sister. I would run anywhere and everywhere. Even as a young adult I habitually wrote down the details of my runs, the distance, overall time, split times, average speed and comments, often with a note to my future self to challenge myself and 'lay down the gauntlet'.

'Great run – pushed it hard from the fifth mile, fast finish. Beat that, Steve!'

When I was 18 my dad was diagnosed with cancer and he fought it for seven long years. I never saw him quit; he never gave in but he eventually passed away in 1998. After that, running became my passion. I thrived on competition either with other runners, at events or with myself and my ongoing commitment and dedication to beat those PBs (personal bests). Life was great but that was all about to change.

So, let's go back to that Sunday, 26 April 2002. It was a rainy afternoon and my car skidded on a patch of water. It aquaplaned and I lost traction on the road. I was no longer in control and the car began turning sideways, heading directly towards a huge metal pole. I braced for impact. As I regained consciousness, I watched as the emergency services arrived one by one: the paramedics, the police, ambulance and fire brigade. Over the next hour and a half they all worked together to cut me free from the twisted wreckage and drag me out. I was strapped tightly to a stretcher and taken in the ambulance, where I was introduced to the two-man crew, both of whom were also called Steve. I felt an instant connection.

At the hospital, the medical staff were fighting for my life. I learned that both of my legs had been crushed from the knee down. My bones were shattered, ligaments torn, my skin and muscles were severely damaged and I'd lost a dangerous amount of blood.

Due to the extreme nature of my injuries, I underwent several life-saving surgeries, including partial amputation of my right leg. The long road to recovery became more apparent when the surgeon informed me, 'You may never walk again.'

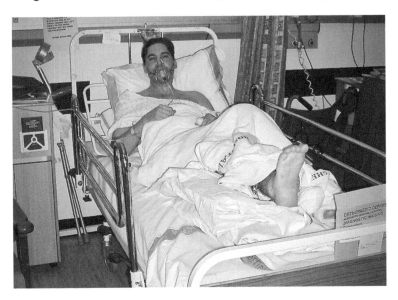

Monday 27 April 2002

Opening my eyes and collecting my thoughts, I slowly realised where I was and what I'd been through. I'd survived but I felt the sting of agonising pain coming from my legs. I could see that my right leg was being held together with a big, round metal cage and was a full 10 cm shorter than my left leg. This was not where I wanted to be and the surgeon's analysis frustrated and angered me. I knew I was broken but I also knew that I wasn't finished. But now I needed to rest.

'Today was a good day because today was the first day that I didn't cry!' These were the words that I wrote in my notebook/ diary four weeks after the accident. They signified to me that something inside had changed and that I wasn't willing to shed any more tears. Or maybe I had run out of tears? I'd entered the stage of acceptance on the 'wave of resilience'. I was starting to focus on what I wanted to achieve rather than where I was and what I wanted to avoid.

The birth of the 'Good to GOLD' concept

As part of an instinctive survival method, I summoned all the learnings, knowledge and experiences of my life up until this point. I put into practice what was now required to recover and pull myself through this period and move forward. I knew what I wanted; I wanted to stand again and walk again and get back to where I was before the accident – of course I did. I wanted to get back to normal. Although as my journey continued, I eventually established that this was impossible. I had to listen to the advice of the practitioners and do everything and anything to move me towards my goals of recovery and I wanted this all immediately. I must admit, I was a little impatient.

'Let's get me standing and I'll take it from there – just give me a pair of damn crutches.'

This might be something that you'd hear in a film as the hero drags themselves out of the hospital bed and back into the fight. Realistically, though, I found that it's a very different scenario.

I relentlessly set myself goals and developed strategies and formed methods to keep moving forward and away from where I was towards where I wanted to be.

October 2003

Once I'd stretched my leg to the right length, the next thing I had to do was to grow 10 cm of bone back as my leg was still being held together by the cage. For over a year I continued to bear weight through my legs through torturous physio, all the time pushing myself. By standing and walking, I encouraged the bone to grow back, until eventually the cage was removed and I was free. My right leg was now the right length but I had a lack of muscle, fragile skin, lack of sensitivity and restricted movement on my ankle, which caused a hell of a lot of pain.

They replaced the four ligaments in my left knee with the ligaments from a pig. Yeah, I know! To be honest, I didn't ask many questions but I did start to feel guilty when eating bacon sandwiches. I had a lack of feeling and movement, nerve spasms, pain and a drop foot, which meant I couldn't lift my left foot up – it just dropped. This was me; this is how it was; these were the cards that I had been dealt and this was how I was playing the game. I'd achieved my goal by standing and walking again. I'd set goals, worked towards them and achieved them. Now looking ahead, I asked myself, 'What's next?'

2004 to 2008

I didn't want the accident to have a detrimental effect on my life so I had to start thinking about what I could do rather than what I couldn't do. I had a new job working as a health and safety manager in the construction industry as well as a new family, with Robert being born and, two years later, Susannah.

I set new goals in the form of swimming, cycling and eventually running. To get my running back after it had been stolen from me for more than seven and a half years was an incredible feeling and gave me the grit and determination to set even more goals.

2009

When I was looking for my next challenge, I found something called a paratriathlon – swimming, cycling and running for disabled athletes. The event was being held in six months' time at a place not far from me called Rother Valley Country Park. I also saw that it was marked as the British Championships and I immediately felt a wave of excitement come over me and a rush of adrenaline through my heart and soul. This was an opportunity that I needed to grab and a competition that I wanted to win. My strategy to achieve resembled and mirrored the same concept that I had used through my rehabilitation. Focusing on what I wanted to achieve and quite literally working towards my GOLD, I set training goals and worked towards them all the way to the event. With the support of my family and friends, who cheered me on through the swim, bike and run, I dug deep, pushed it hard and exhausted every ounce of energy in my body to cross the finish line, winning in my category as the new British champion.

'Congratulations,' said one of the officials. 'You're now the new British champion in your category. Would you like to represent Great Britain?'

'Hell yeah,' I replied – and with that my new goals, pathways and overall journey were set for the next four years.

2010

Wearing the colours of my nation gave me so much pride, pleasure and excitement and now I had the chance to achieve new goals. By grabbing the opportunities presented to me, I knew I could fulfil my passion and love for the sport of triathlon. I once again focused on what I wanted to achieve and I had a new goal: to be the 2011 world champion. Once again, the same winning concept was used throughout my planning, progress and execution towards achieving my goal, my opportunity, my love and my dream. I knew what I wanted and, deep in my soul, why I wanted it. I worked out what I needed to do to win and who would help me to achieve this momentous goal. My timeline of events took me through the year competing in the British Championships, European Championships and onwards to the World Championships.

GOLDEN NUGGET

'Frustration from setbacks creates momentum for the comebacks!'

– Steve Judge

2011

Beijing, China: 'Representing Great Britain, Steve Judge.' I smiled and acknowledged the crowd while trying to appear composed. Now it was all down to me. This was my moment and my time to shine and complete what I'd set out to do. I swam hard but smoothly, pedalled ferociously but in a controlled way and exhausted every ounce of energy in my body during the run. I crossed the finish line as champion of the world. There was euphoria, relief, emotion and exhaustion all rolled into one. This part of my journey was complete: I had achieved my GOLD.

2014 to present day

I retired from international competition having achieved the amazing accolades of five times British champion, one time European champion and two times world champion in the sport of paratriathlon. One of the first things I did was to go back to Scouting, volunteering as a Cub Scout leader at the 6th Eckington Scout Group. I also hold the position of president of Derbyshire Scouts, helping the new generation with fun, challenge, adventure, skills for life and other opportunities. Who knows where those Scout badges will take them later in their lives?

Going forward, I wanted to find new ways to empower people, inspire others and motivate many around the globe. I remember people asking me what I was going to do next and I would stand there, almost in a Superman pose with my hands on my hips, saying in a low and powerful voice, 'I'm going to be a motivational speaker.' Then they would say, 'Wow, how are you going to do that?' And I would reply, 'Erm... I haven't got a clue!' But I knew that if I wanted something enough then I would make it happen. I would make it my focal point, my GOLD; then I could use the same golden concept that had worked before to move towards it and achieve it.

I set goals and seized opportunities in the world of speaking and set up my own business as a professional speaker. I realised that to have longevity on this quest of mine I needed a plan and sustainability. Networking with other businesses, collaborating with other speakers and teaming up with a business coach has enabled me to progress. With the right people I have been able to structure my business goals in coordination with my ultimate GOLD. My business has now expanded to running workshops as well as personal coaching where, with tools and techniques, I help other people find the GOLD in their life and achieve it.

Sharing my messages and inspiring people empowered me to write my Amazon number one bestselling autobiography, *Don't Lean on Your Excuses*, published in 2019. The book allowed me to dig deep and share the full story. Writing this book was a massive achievement and becoming an author was pretty cool too.

What's your GOLD?

So, that's my story and now I hope you can understand why I set myself targets and goals along the way. Using my ambition and self-discipline, I constantly pushed myself away from where I didn't want to be and pulled myself forward towards achievement and ongoing contentment. I now know what it feels like to achieve and it's awesome! The wholesome glow of gratitude unleashes a rush of serotonin and dopamine that makes you stand tall with a beaming smile.

I feel that my purpose is now to share my story and the learnings from it. My ongoing quest is to inspire individuals and teams to visualise what it is that they truly want and desire from this life of theirs – their GOLD. This can be for personal or professional reasons, from small to medium enterprises to large corporations with global impacts. But as with every journey that you set out on, you'll need a map – a 'golden map'.

Chapter 2

Setting your golden map

Find your Polaris

With any journey that you undertake, the first thing you must do is have a map and know where you are on that map. Before you work out or discover where you want to go, you have to find your bearings.

> **GOLDEN NUGGET**
>
> *'You have one lap of this thing called life – if you're not happy with the direction, indicate and change lanes.'*
> – Vicky O'Farrell

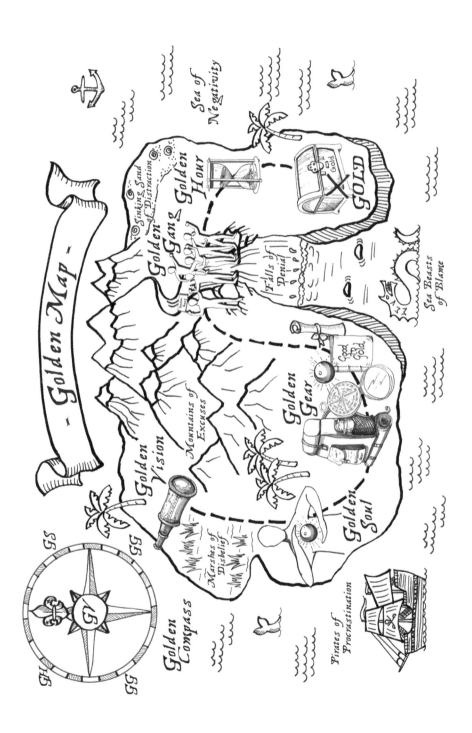

Growing up with the skills I learned from Scouting, I know that before setting off on expeditions you must 'set the map', which means swivel the map until the top lines up with due north. A compass can be used for this but I remember when I was a child my father sat me down to teach me about the constellations. As we sat there under the night sky, we looked up into the vast array of stars scattered across the skyline. My father pointed out the Plough and stated that if you draw an imaginary line through the front two stars it will lead you to the current North Star, Polaris.

He told me, 'Son, when you are lost, look up into the night sky. Find your bearings; focus on the star as your guiding light.'

I remember looking up and seeing the star. 'I see it, Dad, I see the star. It's so bright.'

'Good,' said my dad, 'and that will always be there to guide...'

I interrupted him and screamed, 'and it's flashing and moving. It's getting closer, Dad. I'm scared; it's coming towards us!'

'No, Steve,' he said. 'That's an airplane; you're following an airplane!'

Knowing where you are and who you are before you set off on your journey is essential. Where does your focus go regarding projects, plans and goals? Would you call yourself a high achiever? My definition of a high achiever is 'Someone who is not content with where they are and focuses on what they want to achieve, continually striving forward with ambition and self-discipline.'

The following three exercises will help you find out who you are, where you are and 'set your golden map'.

Exercise 1: what's your focus rating?

So, let's find out what type of a person you are regarding what you focus on. Do you focus on what you want to achieve or do you focus on what you want to avoid?

What follows is an abbreviated version of the focus assessment. You can add up and work out your own score at the end. To complete the comprehensive and detailed online version you can use the link from the references page at the back of the book.

The focus assessment

Read the questions and then tick on the right-hand side which answer you feel best suits you. There is one rule that you must abide by in the completion of this task: don't think too much about the answer – follow your gut, your first instincts.

Q1	When it comes to self-development and intellect, how do you imagine yourself?	Reading books on a daily basis and even quoting from them?		A
		Not having enough time to read any of the books you've recently bought?		B
		Satisfied that you've read a couple of the recommended books. Job done?		C
Q2	When it comes to your financial situation, are you:	Completely happy with your current income and way of life – wanting more is just greedy?		C
		Constantly worrying about not being able to pay the bills, and considering what basics you could cut back on if you needed to?		B
		Always fantasising about how cool it would be to have a little bit more money and what you would do with it?		A

Q3	On Monday morning, do you:	Switch onto automatic pilot during the working week as evenings and weekends are what you live for?		C
		Wake up thinking how much you hate Mondays and just hope the first half of the week doesn't drag?		B
		Wake up thinking about what you are going to accomplish at work in the next week and how good it's going to be?		A
Q4	When it comes to where you work do you:	Accept that where you work doesn't matter; it's what you do when you're there that's important?		C
		Think about how cool and productive your work environment could be with a few adjustments?		A
		Think about how just being at work can drag you down (the room and your desk and sometimes the people)?		B
Q5	You are attending a networking event. Are you:	Feeling that this is going to be a waste of time as nothing much really comes from this kind of event, and you'll probably be stuck with someone that you can't get rid of?		B
		Thinking that 'You've got to be in it to win it' so let's see what happens?		C
		Excited about the prospects that you are going to meet and the potential opportunities that will develop from this event?		A
Q6	Regarding your physical self, do you:	Worry about what you're going to look like on your next holiday and what clothes you're going to wear?		B
		Imagine yourself fit and healthy and looking 'sharp' in the clothes that you want to wear?		A
		Accept that as the years pass your body deteriorates and there's actually no point fighting it.		C

Q7	When it comes to understanding yourself do you:	Feel that checking in on your thoughts and feelings is all a bit New Age 'woo woo' for you? ('I'm fine as I am, thank you very much.')		C
		Worry that as time goes on you'll have more stress and find it harder to move around without some sort of pain?		B
		Imagine being at one with your body, understanding your thoughts and feelings and accepting that you have done all you can do to mitigate any pain that you may have?		A
Q8	When in a loving relationship do you:	Take your relationship for granted?		C
		Think about where your next romantic and fun 'date night' may be with your partner?		A
		Sometimes ponder about how lonely you would be if you didn't have someone in your life?		B

Number of As	Number of Bs	Number of Cs

Calculating your focus assessment rating

When you have finished, add up all the As, Bs and Cs that you ticked. Then convert those into your total score using the following values:

- A = 3 points
- B = 2 points
- C = 1 point.

Now convert your total score into your focus assessment rating by using the following formula:

**Your total score divided by 2.4 = FAR_____
(focus assessment rating)**

Analysis of results

A FAR between 0 and 7 will signify that you generally focus on avoidance. With a FAR between 8 and 10, you generally focus on achievement.

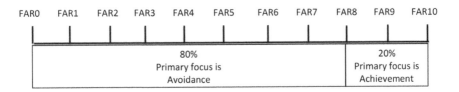

If you're in the 20 per cent section and are already focusing on what you will achieve, then this book is perfect for you, especially Chapter 3. You are clearly already in tune with the concept but also the following chapters will enhance your vision in working towards the GOLD in your life.

If you're in the 80 per cent section, then this book will empower you to adjust your focus and understand the concept of focusing more on what you want to achieve in order for you to succeed. The stories in Chapter 3 will show how this technique helped me throughout my journey and continues to do so.

Exercise 2: what's your achiever assessment rating?

So, what if you focus on your dreams and your vision? What difference does that make? What we really want to know is this: are you a high achiever are not? Is there any correlation between the things you do and what you achieve? Do you want to be a high achiever? Do you think you already are? Where do you think you are as an individual? What about the members of your team, department business or corporation?

Here's an abbreviated version of the assessment for you to complete now. You can add up and work out your own score at the end.

The achiever assessment

Read the questions and then tick on the right-hand side which answer you feel best suits you. Once again, the same rule applies: don't think too much about your answer. Follow your gut and your first instincts.

1	When do I want to achieve it? Well, what time is it now?	Agree strongly		A
		Agree		B
		Neither agree nor disagree		C
		Disagree		D
		Disagree strongly		E
2	The word yes comes out waaay too quickly after I hear the word opportunity.	Agree strongly		A
		Agree		B
		Neither agree nor disagree		C
		Disagree		D
		Disagree strongly		E
3	YES! I achieved a massive goal. Now what? What's next?	Agree strongly		A
		Agree		B
		Neither agree nor disagree		C
		Disagree		D
		Disagree strongly		E
4	The second best day of my life: discovering personal development books on audio. The best day of my life: discovering I could play audiobooks at double the speed.	Agree strongly		A
		Agree		B
		Neither agree nor disagree		C
		Disagree		D
		Disagree strongly		E
5	Belief enables me to climb those mountains before I even take a step.	Agree strongly		A
		Agree		B
		Neither agree nor disagree		C
		Disagree		D
		Disagree strongly		E

6	20-minute meditation session done. Tomorrow, let's go for 40.	Agree highly	A
		Agree	B
		Neither agree nor disagree	C
		Disagree	D
		Disagree strongly	E
7	Failure to launch. Damn you, inner perfectionist!	Agree strongly	A
		Agree	B
		Neither agree nor disagree	C
		Disagree	D
		Disagree strongly	E
8	If we get the timing right we can go to both parties and then follow on to the theatre.	Agree strongly	A
		Agree	B
		Neither agree nor disagree	C
		Disagree	D
		Disagree strongly	E

Number of As	Number of Bs	Number of Cs	Number of Ds	Number of Es

Calculating your achiever assessment rating

When you have finished, add up all the As, Bs, Cs, Ds and Es that you ticked. Convert these into your total score using the following values:

- A = 5 points
- B = 4 points
- C = 3 points
- D = 2 points
- E = 1 point.

Now convert your total score into your achiever assessment rating by using the following formula:

Your total score divided by 4 = AAR_____ (achiever assessment rating)

Analysis of results

Once again, you'll have worked out a rating that relates to the achiever assessment rating scale image below. The higher the rating, the more of a high achiever you are with a rating of AAR10 being the highest.

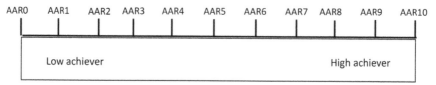

No matter what score you have for this exercise, this book will help you to grow and retain your achiever rating. Knowing what you want is important but in Chapter 4 you'll find out why you want it. Knowing your 'golden soul' will keep you motivated to keep going and ask the question 'How do I get it, then?' That question is then answered throughout the rest of the book.

> **GOLDEN NUGGET**
> *'You are the average of the five people you spend the most time with.'*
> – Jim Rohn

Knowing me, knowing you

So now you have two sets of results from your assessments – but what about everybody else in your team or department? When working towards a goal with others, it's important to share your results with them and equally important to know what their assessment scores are. Who are they and what elements of their life are they focusing on to achieve them? More than likely you'll have a mixture of results, which is fine because now you have the knowledge. This knowledge brings awareness and from that you can take action to move and improve.

The results from these assessments generally show that high

achievers focus more on what they want to achieve than what they want to avoid. So how did your results and the results of your team compare to this statement? Knowing where you are is powerful information because now you have a benchmark – a starting point so that you and your golden gang can all move forward in unison and understanding. This book will help and explain how the low-scoring recipients can improve their rating and equally how the higher-scoring recipients can enhance what they already have. Ultimately, this book will empower everybody to move forward with learnings and exercises to become the high achievers that they want to be.

> **GOLDEN NUGGET**
> 'Every day we have a choice. Complain about the unfairness and feel bitter. Or proclaim our self-determined right to create every day as we choose it to be. And smile.'
> – Rob Pickering

Don't die with the song still inside you

The thing that frustrates me is people saying that they want to do things but never doing anything about it. These are usually the same people who call other, more successful people lucky! And yet these are the people who are not living their own life to their fullest and on top of that they're complaining about it. So, let me ask you, how are things? Are you good? OK? So-so? Or are you great, fantastic or awesome? How's work going? How's your business – is it good? How are your relationships? How is your wealth or your fitness? How is your health? How do you feel? Are you happy?

Often, these simple questions bring back answers such as 'Yeah, I'm OK' or 'Ah well, work's work; it pays the bills' or even

'Yeah, it's so-so – could be better.'

For me these aren't the answers that anybody should be giving. The answers I'm looking for are 'Things are fantastic/ awesome/brilliant.' Wouldn't it be good if your work brought you satisfaction or even enjoyment? How good would it be to have contented employees or a happy workforce? Wouldn't it be nice if your relationships brought you happiness or love? How great would it be if your health, wealth and fitness were brilliant? If you're not getting any of these answers, then don't you feel you should be asking yourself 'Why not?'

Where are you now?

In order to move towards what you truly want, you need to know where you stand now. Knowing where you are will help you to focus on the areas that you may need to concentrate on. The areas that, when you target and deal with them, will bring you joy, happiness and a glowing aura. If you're working in a team or department then how are all the employees? How are the staff? Where are they now, not only in reference to work but in all aspects of their lives? Because in one way or another they are all connected. You might consider emotional, physical, financial, intellectual, occupational, environmental, social and spiritual aspects of your life. It's important to know what it is that you're working towards as this will lead you towards your joy and your self-actualisation.

Eric Garton and Michael Mankins wrote in *Harvard Business Review* (2015) that 'Employees who are inspired are 58 per cent more productive than engaged employees and 125 per cent more productive than merely satisfied employees.'

So, are your employees satisfied? Are your employees engaged? Are your employees inspired?

Exercise 3: your 360° wheel of life

Where are you now? What's your primary goal? When I think back to my time in hospital all I really wanted and needed was to get better and get out of hospital. My focus wasn't on my social life or my financial situation. I'd gone into survival mode and all that mattered to me was my health. I feel that when it comes down to health, you can't have a much bigger drive, surely? I was fighting for my life, and I can remember that my goal was simply to eat food for energy. I felt so weak, I didn't even have the energy to lift the food into my mouth. Chewing the food was a chore and gulping it down and swallowing was an effort. Five minutes of this and I was exhausted and had to rest. Can you imagine how frustrating that was for me, knowing what I had to do to survive but struggling to achieve those simple tasks? However, that was my goal and that's what I worked towards, day by day, week by week, getting the energy to take me forward.

So obvious!

Sometimes it's obvious what your goal is. Maybe you're in a tight financial situation and you need to get out of serious debt before the bailiffs come knocking on your door. Maybe you hate your job and the thought of going to work summons up the fear inside you, every day, especially on Mondays. Maybe a trusted friend or even a doctor has recommended a weight loss strategy for you due to diagnosed life-threatening health issues. Situations like these are horrible but they help you prioritise what you need to do and what to concentrate all your efforts on to move forward.

Not so obvious...

What can be harder to establish is when you're not too sure exactly what improvements you want in your life but you just want to be 'happier' or 'less stressed'. Addressing these statements involves digging a little deeper into all aspects of your life as they are all connected.

In situations like these, I always start off my one-to-one coaching sessions by asking the client, 'Where are you now?' When a new client asks me to help them with achieving their goals, one of the first things I ask is, 'Where are you now in relation to the goal you want to achieve?' I ask the same question when I'm working with a group of people or a whole company.

By understanding where each individual team member is, you'll understand where the team or department are. The awareness of the individual's status will inform as well as affect the overall status of the team, department and company.

A great tool that I use in my workshops is called the 'wheel of life'. This was originally created by Paul J. Meyer and is now used globally by coaches. When my delegates complete this wheel they not only get a benchmark of where they are in their current situation but they can also see the areas where they need improvements, even if they're small, incremental ones. By carrying out this exercise you will find out where you are in your life right now. This will help you set your golden map in order to start plotting your journey that will take you from your good to your GOLD.

I'd like you to rate your level of satisfaction in the eight areas of your life with zero (centre of the wheel) equating to not satisfied and 10 (outer circumference of the wheel) equating to highly satisfied.

Two rules apply for the completion of this task: don't lie about or exaggerate your rating; and don't think too much about the rating you're giving – follow your gut and your first instincts.

Are you ready? Then let's go.

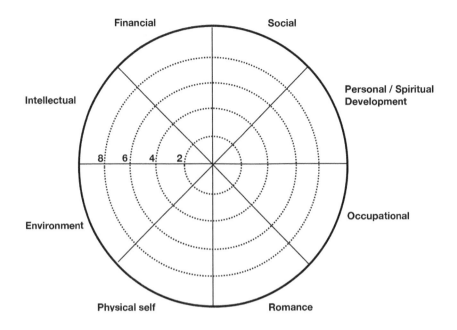

Each section relates to an area in your life, so you need to rate your current level of satisfaction in each of them from 0 to 10 (0 = low, 10 = fantastic).

- **Social**: hobbies, friends, lifestyle, relaxing, family, community, fun.
- **Personal/spiritual development**: understanding yourself, wellness, religious beliefs, self-worth.
- **Occupational**: career, work, job, business.
- **Romance**: intimacy, love, relationships.
- **Physical self**: fitness, health, self-care, diet/nutrition, sleep.
- **Environment**: home/office, living area. Does it give or take energy? Does it cause stress? Think about relatives, colleagues, neighbours.
- **Intellectual**: academic, self-development, understanding, education, reading.
- **Financial**: money, savings, earnings, investments.

Once you have rated each section then shade in the area from the centre of the circle to the line that you have stipulated as your level. Basically, the more shading you do, the higher your satisfaction levels.

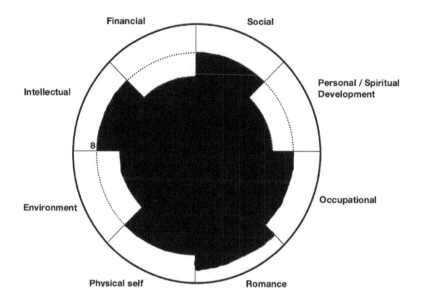

Exercise 4: your rating list

Reviewing your results is a two-step process.

Step 1

The first step is to see how balanced your life is. Each element in your life is connected and affected by the other elements, so balance is the key to smoothing the journey. If you imagine the shaded area as a wheel, then how smooth would your journey be using that wheel? The goals that need to be set are the ones that will smooth out the roundness of the wheel.

Sometimes the temptation is to set goals in all eight areas of your life. I totally understand this because I love setting goals to push me towards improvement, but in fact this can overload you. Even if you decide to set multiple goals, I'd strongly advise you to decide on your primary goals. Just choose two or three areas of your life to set as your goals.

Using the grid template below, make a list of your results starting with the lowest score at the top.

Rating	Element of life
1 (lowest)	
2	
3	
4	
5	
6	
7	
8	

You've now created a list that signifies the areas of your life where you should potentially set goals.

Step 2

The second step is more about imagining what a 10 out of 10 would look like in each of the areas. What would it mean to you, what does that feel like and what does it look like? I'm just planting a seed here as I'll cover this fully in the next chapter.

What you have in front of you now is a clear and visible benchmark from which you can work. But it's not all about where you are; it's about where you want to be. Seeing where you are in your current life will enable you to start focusing on where you truly want to be. Start thinking about what a fully shaded circle would look and feel like for you. Share your thoughts with people and encourage others who have carried out this exercise to express what a balanced wheel would look like for them. Where would they be, what would they be doing and who are they with? With regard to your vision, picture yourself in that future euphoria of bliss and happiness. This is your GOLD and this is what you'll be working towards.

Watch out, though! As you start imagining the future that you truly deserve, your survival brain will kick into action by asking lots of serious and practical questions such as:

- 'How will you get there?'
- 'Who will help me? I don't have time!'
- 'Why am I even doing this?'

Barriers and obstacles will be placed in your way by yourself, by others or by circumstances that will challenge you before you've even started on your journey. But don't worry, because this book will act as a guide that will help you. It will support and empower you on your journey by sharing the five winning strategies that are needed to achieve. These strategies form the metaphorical golden compass, which will give you, and those who join you, direction on this journey to take you from where you are to where you want to be – from your good to your GOLD.

So, let's confirm what it is you truly want. Your golden map has been set and in the next chapter you'll confirm and visualise what you're working towards and where the map is leading you. You'll discover what exactly your GOLD is. The most extraordinary life you've ever imagined is there for you and now it's time to take it – it's yours.

Chapter 3
Your golden vision

GOLDEN NUGGET
'Start with the end in mind.'
– Stephen Covey, *The 7 Habits of Highly Effective People*

There seems to be one major principle that separates high achievers from everyone else and this realisation blew my mind. Consequently, and importantly, this forms the first strategy out of the five and it's all about knowing what you want and how you see it and focus on it. Every journey needs a destination, an end point, something to head for. The purpose of this book is to help you to know what it is that you want. What is that ultimate goal that you want to achieve; what is the opportunity that you want to seize and grab with both hands and make happen? What is it that you love and makes you glow inside and that you want more of? What ultimately is your dream? When you close your eyes and see yourself in the future in a happy state, what is it that you're doing, where are you, who are you with?

In my journey all of these questions were answered by me establishing what my GOLD was not only by thinking about it but also by seeing it, and that's when the magic really happened.

Drawing my vision

As I recovered from my accident in the orthopaedic ward, I used a notebook and pen to monitor what medication I needed at what time and the information the doctors, surgeons, nurses and physios had given me. I had trouble knowing what day it was let alone what complicated aspects of my injuries were being considered. The notebook slowly turned into some sort of diary or journal as it was useful for benchmarking. When I felt terrible on a particular day, I could guarantee that if I turned back a couple of pages, I'd felt even worse, so to me that was progress. After about four weeks on this treadmill, my tears had stopped but my anger had not. Looking down at my legs I concluded that I would never run again. My joy and my passion and my release had been taken from me. My wings had been clipped and were now gone.

> **GOLDEN NUGGET**
>
> *'If you can't fly, run. If you can't run, walk. If you can't walk, crawl, but by all means, keep moving.'*
> – Martin Luther King Jr

I lay there in the hospital bed staring at the ceiling and thinking of all of the things that I wanted to do. My impatience and frustration made me very anxious. It was like a spring inside me was being coiled tighter and tighter, squeezing my lungs and making my heart beat faster. My inner white tiger was awake and now he was scratching on the cage door ready to pounce.

I grabbed my pen and notebook and started sketching. I started drawing a picture of myself, not in the state that I was in but a future state. I was standing up, tall and straight and strong. At the side of me were my discarded crutches. I was standing on top of a small mountain looking forward towards the future. As I stared at the drawing my eyes started to well up and my mouth began to quiver. I wanted it... I wanted it now. I had an urge to throw off the bed covers and drag myself out of the hospital like you see people do in the movies. Seeing the thing that I really wanted sparked a flame inside me. Staring at the image, I believed that I could do it and inside I knew that I was going to achieve it. In the hospital, the image that I had drawn helped me to believe what was possible. I was surrounded with people in wheelchairs and patients who'd had amputations. I didn't want to be where I was; I had a vision and knew what I wanted. I was hungry for it. I just needed to start working towards it, now.

Connecting with my reticular activating system

Having that image gave me something positive to focus on but little did I realise that I'd created my own future; now it was just a matter of time. Well, not just time – also lots of hard work, dedication and commitment. But ultimately, I knew where I was heading and I knew my destination.

I'd also done more than that. I'd activated a filter system in my brain that would help me to become aware of the opportunities that I needed to achieve my GOLD. It's called the reticular activating system or RAS (Science Direct 2022).

To be honest, I don't fully understand the science behind this, but this is how it affects the brain. First, consider the fact that more than 20 million pieces of information infiltrate your brain every day. These come in the form of things you see, hear, touch, smell, taste or feel. Your subconscious acknowledges all these inputs but, to avoid overloading your conscious mind, the RAS will filter for what is deemed important and what is not. For this reason, you can sometimes go through a whole day not acknowledging certain things, almost as if you are walking around with blinkers on. You may miss out on things that everybody else sees because to you at that time they are insignificant.

This is quite normal and nothing to be ashamed of, but how would you like to program your RAS so that you're more in control of the process; you pick up on the things that you do want to see and ignore all the things you're not bothered about? Surely that would be more efficient. You could even compare it to a superpower! Or maybe that's just me. Anyway, that's exactly what visualisation is. By visualising what you want in detail, your brain will start seeing and hearing things that relate to that vision. It will make connections with what people are saying and you'll focus on things associated with your vision. You will be programming your RAS to notice all the important and useful bits of information that will take you in the direction of your goal and ultimately your GOLD.

You may have already done something like this in different situations. For example, if you were thinking about buying a certain type of car in the colour red, then over the next couple of days all you'll see is lots of similar red cars on the road. Or maybe you're thinking of a certain song and then you hear that song on the radio or playing somewhere.

You may find yourself saying things such as:

- 'Well, that's a coincidence.'
- 'What a stroke of luck.'
- 'Wow, that must be fate.'

Let me tell you, there is no such thing as luck or fate and there is no such thing as coincidence. You make your own luck. Opportunities are around us all the time; you've got to see them, hear them and even smell them and then do something about them. Grab hold of them with both hands and take action. You must reset and program your RAS every single day to focus on the things that you want in your life. I do this every morning as part of my golden morning routine, more of which later.

Bringing my picture to life

Later, as an elite athlete representing my country and achieving British champion status, I was once again setting goals and working towards them. My GOLD quickly became my passion to become the world champion. I knew exactly what to do – I needed to draw a picture. Even at this stage I knew nothing about how it connected with my RAS but what I did know is that it worked through my rehabilitation and I was willing to give it another go.

Getting my dream and desires out of my head so that I could see them inspired me and stoked the fire from within to keep training and pushing and grabbing those opportunities. The image was me crossing the finish line wearing my GB kit, hands in the air, crowd cheering and a massive sign saying 'World Championships'. I spent a bit more time on the picture and even added colour to bring it to life.

The picture was placed in my bathroom, so I'd see it every day but I'd also see it in my mind when I was training, especially when I was on my rowing machine. I used to zone out in a meditative state as I pushed my body to hell and back. My mind expanded the vision to include the whole race from start to finish, ending in me crossing the finish line and beaming a smile through the dripping sweat. It worked so well and empowered my inner being, heart and soul, rattling the cage of my inner white tiger. I actually felt what it was going to be like, so I wanted it even more!

Neg med

Visualisation is a powerful tool that's used by many successful high achievers. The more you do it, the more effective it will become. The trick is to ensure that your visualisation is positive in every possible way. In my visualisation as an athlete, I never got punched or kicked in the mass swim start. I never got a puncture on the bike and I never put my shoes on the wrong feet in transition. The brain will naturally try to bring in negative thoughts and this is not the time or place for them, so what I do is I create a time and a place for them. I call this time 'neg med', which stands for negative meditation. It's not really meditation but I think neg med sounds good, so bear with me. In a way, neg med is the opposite of visualisation. It's the nemesis or the alter ego, the yin to the yang, the Darth Vader to Obi-Wan Kenobi. In my neg med session, I allow myself to bring out all my negative thoughts. I dig down deep to all those things that I've buried that would block me on my journey.

A word of warning: this can be quite intense, but better out than in, as my mum always says.

When I do my neg med, I ask myself the simple question 'What's making me nervous?' I guess I'm asking my gut or inner being and allowing myself to release my anxiety for the greater good. What I mean by that is once I've accepted all this built-up tension full of negative thoughts and nervousness, I can do something about it. I now have a list of things that I need to deal with, work on or conquer. These things could have been physical barriers or mental blocks but now I know what they are. Now I can deal with them and get them sorted out, get rid of them to clear the path for me to continue on my journey towards my GOLD.

As an athlete this might have included thoughts such as 'I don't know the cycle route!' The answer might be 'OK, so let's Google Earth it – maybe arrive early and drive round it or even better cycle round it.' Or it might be 'What if my goggles leak in the race and let in water?' One answer might be 'OK, let's go swimming and make my goggles leak and find out what to do in that situation.' (The solution to this was to put them round my neck or throw them away. I preferred the former as throwing away my goggles seemed a bit extreme – an expensive solution and bad for the environment.)

I currently use neg med in my work as a professional speaker.

What makes me nervous is arriving on time and checking that all the technology works. Because I know this makes me nervous, I always plan to arrive super early and where possible the day before, giving me ample time to 'check the tech' and make sure I'm happy with the set-up. Once I've sorted out my demons it allows me to have a positive and fulfilling visualisation session. Yes, I do visualisation before my speaking engagements because it gives me so much inner fulfilment and confidence for the event ahead. After this I open my eyes knowing how amazing it's going to be and I can't wait to make it happen.

My BSG

When I started out as a motivational speaker, I shared my story to small rooms of people, including local church groups, rotary clubs and a few schools. It was nice but I wanted more. In my heart I wanted to inspire and empower thousands of people on a big stage with a big audience. For me this became my business GOLD so I knew exactly what to do and that was to draw a picture! But this time I drew two pictures. I split the page in half and on the left-hand side I drew a picture of where I was, as a benchmark. I drew a picture of me happy and presenting in front of maybe 20 or 30 people in a small, well-lit room that could have even been a church hall or small conference room. There was a pop-up projector screen at the front and I'm wearing my dark blue jeans and open collar white shirt as my stylist had suggested that this is a good look for me. (I'll say more about my stylist in Chapter 6.)

My stylist also said that I'd look good in a dark blue three-piece suit but at that time I couldn't afford a new suit; what I had was fine. Over on the other side of the sheet the picture in contrast was a lot more magnificent and in technicolour. I'm standing there, arms aloft, on a big stage, with a big screen behind me. In front of me is an audience of a thousand or more. There are lights shining down on me and I'm wearing a stylish blue suit. I'm even wearing a cool head mic, like the one Madonna made famous in the late 1980s. As I looked at the image I'd sketched on the right I got excited and smiled. I said to myself, 'I want it. I want it now', speaking as if I already had the gig booked or knew how I was going to get there. Let's be clear, I had absolutely no idea how I was going to make it happen but I knew by now that if I wanted something enough, if I was passionate about it in my soul and could conceive the end result, then I would believe it. And if I believed that I could make it, then I could push myself forward and achieve it. With that I wrote three phrases connecting the left image to the one on the right: *conceive it, believe it and achieve it*. This would become the three-phrase mantra that would take me from good to GOLD in my speaker business.

The picture was given a prominent position on the noticeboard in my office, which I referred to as my vision board. Over the next couple of years, I worked hard every day to manifest it in my business. I called this vision (my GOLD) my 'blue suit gig' or BSG. Being aware of my vision triggered my RAS and I was able to see and grab opportunities. Eventually I teamed up with a business coach from ActionCOACH to help and support me on my journey. I hungrily learned and absorbed the skills required to run a business, from marketing to lead generation, sales funnels and conversion, networking like a ninja to make the contacts and ignite the conversations and referrals that would take me and my business forward. I travelled round the UK taking the speaking opportunities that could potentially lead to others, opening new avenues and enquiries to achieve my BSG. I put in hours rehearsing and perfecting my presentation skills with the Professional Speaking Association by pushing myself out of my comfort zone, entering competitions, showcases and assessment sessions. I took on board the floods of feedback that I received but knew that this was what I had to do to achieve my goal, my dream and the vision that I had drawn.

And then one day I got a phone call – an enquiry for a speaking gig. I frantically rustled the papers around my desk, grabbing the sales script that I had prepared for just this occasion. As we went through the 'building rapport' stage and moved on to the 'details and arrangements' stage I was able to probe for more information.

'And the audience, tell me about the audience,' I enquired. 'Thousands, you say? Yes, that's absolutely fine,' I said, 'absolutely fine.' I could feel my heart beating faster and I was thinking that this could be the one. 'And what's the venue like? Oh! So, a big stage, I'd imagine? And some big lights will be needed for that size of venue, with presumably a big screen to share my slides? Wow, that is a big screen,' I replied, smiling down the phone.

'This is it,' I thought to myself. 'This is my BSG.'

The conversation continued. 'So, can we talk about the budget?' After a few exchanges I replied, a little bit flustered, 'Er, yes. I can accommodate that budget.' By now I was beaming and my hand was shaking as it was a done deal and secured with a virtual handshake. We confirmed various details and requirements and then, just before we hung up, I asked one final question: 'So, I was just wondering, when I'm on stage, will I be able to wear one of those head mics?' I waited with bated breath for the response as for me this was the final piece of the jigsaw. 'You'll make that possible, will you? That's fantastic, brilliant. Thank you so much!'

After the call, I punched the air in triumph and danced round the room like a lunatic saying over and over again, 'I've got my BSG, I've got my BSG!' I was so happy, excited and relieved that after all the hard work, dedication and commitment that I'd put in over the years I'd finally made it; I'd achieved my GOLD. The next phone call I made was to my partner Jo, who'd supported me on this journey and knew what this meant to me. I said, 'We're going shopping.' She said, 'Oh lovely, what are we buying?' And I said, with a smile, 'A new blue suit.'

Feel the image

In this scenario, it was interesting that I'd drawn two pictures and included so much detail in the second picture. Drawing the first picture was a benchmark for me as it really stated where I was in relation to my dream. It reminded me of where I wanted to move from, which wasn't necessarily a bad or unhappy place but just a place I wasn't content with. Another crucial part of the drawing exercise was the fact that I was actually there within each scenario. I was in the image on the left and the image on the right. More than that, I could see that it was me, I was recognisable, with my distinctive smile and floppy fringe. If I hadn't made it clearly me then my brain could have repelled the image on the right as a limiting belief and seen a stranger. It would have struggled with the concept that I could ever achieve anything as big and bold as what I'd imagined. The brain can be fickle like that. I also added a lot of detail and colour to the image on the right, encouraging me to focus on this more and to help my brain to believe the whole concept.

As author Sam Ashken (2016) explains, we humans see everything in 2D through our eyes and then our brain pretty much guesses and works out through experience what things might look like in 3D and accepts the concept. If you were to see a 2D image of a cup with a handle, you would naturally presume that it was a circular vessel that you could pick up and drink from. If there was more detail, such as a reflection or shadow on the image, then this would enhance your belief even more. In this sense I was doing the same. I wanted my brain to believe in the image that I had drawn. As I added colour and a lot more detail to the picture, my brain recognised, understood and could conceive the image better. This is exactly what I wanted so that when I closed my eyes the image would truly come to life. My palms would feel sweaty from the nervous excitement of standing on the stage in front of thousands of people. I would feel the heat from the lights shining down on me and I'd hear the applause from the crowd. I would be smiling as I opened my eyes, whispering the words, 'I want it; I want it now.'

Experience the image

I've used this method for various goals in my life and it gives me something to focus on, something that I wholeheartedly want. As I look at my picture my brain starts piecing together the separate parts of the image as everything is connected. To take this further I close my eyes and bring it to life by adding more detail, moving images and sounds and even feelings. I can create a dream of what this will be like in the future and how it will make me and others feel. The more realistically I do this, the more my brain believes that it's true and ignites passion, euphoria and excitement within me. At this point I open my eyes and bring myself back to reality but now I have the belief that I will achieve my vision – and more than that, I'm hungry for it. I want that feeling I've just had and I will do anything and everything to make it happen.

In doing all this I've reprogrammed my brain and specifically my RAS regarding what I want and also what I need to look out for to bring the dream alive. The 20 million pieces of data input will now subconsciously be filtered down so that I see, hear and feel those opportunities that will take me towards my dream and my vision.

What's your vision?

So, what about you: what's your golden vision? Visualisation is so powerful and is such a useful tool. It will help you to conceive, believe and achieve your goal and it's free and easy to do. In fact a lot of us do it every day but we call it daydreaming or fantasising. In fact, it's just like that; you just need to hone it a little bit and give it a bit more structure and detail. It's like those conversations about what you'd do if you won the lottery. 'Oh, I'd buy a big car and a big house and we'd go away on fantastic holidays. I wouldn't have to work so much so I'd spend my time shopping or playing golf. I may even do some charity work, you know, to keep myself busy and give something back. Maybe hire a personal trainer and a chef and get myself in shape.'

If you've ever said anything along these lines, then you're in the right place to visualise your goals because that's exactly what they are. To make your visualisation really come to life you need to see it in more detail, for example:

- What type of car do you want?
- What colour is it?
- Who's in the car with you?

- Where are you driving?
- What tune is playing while you're driving?

Be free with your answers as it's just a visualisation so you can have any car you want. If you want to go shopping:

- Where are you shopping? New York, Milan, London?
- What are you buying?
- Can you feel it in your hands, turn it around and feel the quality?

You can be anywhere in the world; you are not restricted by common sense at this moment in time.

If you want to do some charity work and give something back:

- Who's this for – is it in your local community or an international charity?
- How does it make you feel knowing that you are making a difference?
- Big yourself up and enjoy the accolade that you're receiving within your vision.

The point is that visualisation can be fun and exciting and the more detail you can feed your brain, the more it actually believes that it's true. For this to work, this part is crucial. As much as I encourage this initially as an individual exercise, I've also run group sessions with teams and departments so that an overall image for the company is achieved. On one occasion, once the preliminary picture was created a local artist was contracted to recreate the image on the wall of the reception area. Every day the staff and clients would see the image of their vision and mission.

Feel free to carry out this exercise in the book and maybe take a photo of the finished product. Alternatively, go to the Resources section (on page 137) where there is a link for you to download and print off an original template. Your completed exercise can then be displayed where you will see it on a daily basis.

Exercise 5: draw your vision

Are you ready? Then let's go.

Be aware of your vision,
seize opportunities

Where you are now?   Your Golden Vision - Your GOLD

On the sheet there are two areas for you to draw. Before you start saying that you can't draw, let me tell you that it's not all about the quality of the drawing – stick people will do. Don't start leaning on your excuses. The first image you draw will be a representation of your '360° wheel of life' from the exercise that you completed at the end of Chapter 2. The picture doesn't have to represent every one of the eight aspects, just the ones where you most want a change to happen. Make sure you can see yourself in the picture and that it represents you in some way. Maybe you wear glasses or have long hair or wear a certain colour top. In a business or career environment I encourage the participants of my workshops to concentrate on the aspects that are strongly associated with where the team, department or company may want to see improvement or change. For example, this may be the aspects of occupational or personal development rather than romance or social matters.

Add in as much detail as you can and where possible refrain from using words. I do understand that not everybody is a visual person and some may be more auditory or kinaesthetic but for this exercise a visual representation is best. The detail can also include the weather, as this is a common literary device to portray human emotions and mood. Maybe in your first picture the sun is just hidden behind a cloud or maybe there are some dark clouds, rain or even thunder and lightning.

Once you have drawn yourself in this scenario then the next part is the fun stuff. Moving over to the right-hand side of the page, draw a picture of yourself in the future. Once again from the exercise in Chapter 2, what would a full 10 out of 10 look like to you? It's completely open whether this is one year, five years or 10 years in the future – it really doesn't matter. The point is to let your inhibitions go as they only restrain, suppress and block, so draw your fantasies and dreams and what you really, really want. It's just a drawing, so go crazy. Make sure that you can see yourself in the image. As I mentioned earlier on, visualising yourself in a perfect future scenario is sometimes difficult for your brain to accept, so it's particularly important to clarify that this is you and no one else.

The exercise works best if you mirror the aspects that you drew on the left-hand side of the sheet. For example, if you drew a picture depicting that you were unhappy, stressed and overworked in your job then this new picture should portray the perfect scenario that you aspire to achieve in your job, career or occupation. Put some details into the picture. For example, if you want lots of money, what would you spend the money on? Then draw it. If you want to live in a big house, then who is in the house with you? If you're struggling to think of anything, then imagine what kind of happiness would enable you to flourish. Maybe you have a new qualification or your business is thriving and growing and you can have more time off work. Maybe you've lost weight or you're fitter or stronger. There are no constraints – just draw what you want.

The final thing I suggest to my workshop delegates is to add some colour to the picture and really bring it to life. Leave that dismal left-hand image in black and white where it belongs. Instead let's bring the visualisation on the right to life with bright colours and a beautiful outlook that is shining and alive.

So, there you have it – your vision of the future. A picture of who you want to be and what you want to achieve along with who you'd like to do it with. These are the basic elements of your visualisation, something for you to look at.

Conceive it.

Believe it.

Achieve it.

You know, there will be barriers, obstacles and pitfalls on this journey and at times it will be hard to stay focused and motivated. To empower you to push through these phases it's extremely important to know your true purpose and question yourself as to why on earth you are doing all this. This is called your 'golden soul' and the next chapter will enable you to find yours. Knowing mine was crucial for various parts of my journey. So, when someone suggested that I should quit, I knew I needed to fight on.

Chapter 4

Your golden soul

'How do you stay motivated?' is a common question that I'm asked during my public speaking, workshops and coaching. It's a good question because people really want to know how *they* can stay motivated. Knowing what you want is great but I understand that sometimes it's challenging to stay on the path that will lead you and your team to your GOLD. There are lots of tools that can be used to keep you motivated, such as the golden vision picture that you've drawn or turning your noticeboard or blank wall into a vision board or maybe even setting up a music playlist. (See later in the chapter as well as the resources page at the end of the book for more about music for this purpose.) There are books, poems and quotes that can keep you focused and inspired but all these are connected by one thing and that is knowing what your golden soul is. Your golden soul will connect your goals with your dreams at an emotional level to truly understand what's driving you on this journey of yours.

GOLDEN NUGGET

'Remember that wherever your heart is, there you will find your treasure.'
— Paulo Coelho, *The Alchemist*

Knowing the emotion behind your GOLD is strongly connected to knowing your purpose or your 'why' (more on this below). For me it was an essential part of my success in going from wheelchair to world champion and beyond. Not just to know where I was going but to know my why deep down in my soul, my golden soul. This became most critical when I was faced with physical or mental barriers. Knowing my golden soul empowered me not to lean on my excuses but instead to turn my excuses into challenges and push forward.

Emotional guidance

By knowing and using our emotional state we can energise ourselves and move ourselves forward. It's almost as though the word emotion derives from the two words energy and motion. The way I like to look at it is that if you put emotion behind your GOLD, if you know why you are working towards it, then this will energise your golden soul and motivate you to take action.

> **GOLDEN NUGGET**
> *'Involving emotion in your undertaking will generate energy and motion on your journey.'*
> – Steve Judge

Tightening my nuts

My consultant once said to me, 'Mr Judge, if you are unable to straighten your leg, there will be repercussions. For one, you will walk with a limp for the rest of your life.' These words shocked me and sparked anger and fear, and that's what I needed to take extreme action. It was my right leg that had already been subjected to the bone lengthening, with stretched tendons and ligaments. Now the leg wouldn't straighten at the knee. Talk about being knocked down and having to pick myself up again and again and again!

I jumped into action by buying a protractor to measure my knee bend and give me some sort of benchmark before the physio started. I say physio but it was more self-inflicted torture and persecution. The 30-minute session that I subjected my knee to through gritted teeth three times a day always left me out of breath and exhausted. The pain would drain me and then, with shaky and sweaty hands, I'd eventually place the protractor in position and record the small incremental results gained.

> **GOLDEN NUGGET**
> *'Physio is something that you do, not something that you get.'*
> – Steve Judge

It was important to me to know deep in my soul why I was doing all this. It had been explained to me that without a straight leg I wouldn't be able to bear weight as my knee would buckle. If I couldn't bear weight, then my bone wouldn't grow back strong and if my bone didn't do that then initially I couldn't have the cage taken off my leg. Consequently, a bent knee would cause a limp, which would lead to hip and back issues and further disabling health implications. 'Wow, OK, I get it,' I used to hear myself saying. 'I need a straight leg!'

It wasn't just my goal of having a straight leg; it was giving my future self the satisfaction that I was doing absolutely anything and everything possible so that I would have the best chance of full recovery. That's what I really wanted: to get back to where I was and prove that the accident was nothing more than a blip or a slight glitch on my journey.

I could hear my future self expressing its feelings about possible outcomes if I didn't keep going. 'You idiot... look at what I've got because of what you didn't do, because you didn't want the pain or couldn't commit the time! Look at what I'm left with! Loser.'

I continued with stubbornness, dedication, tears and pain but after three long months of leg straightening, the results showed that it hadn't worked. I was broken. I was in a dark place and felt like quitting, but now my future self was there with an outstretched hand, encouraging me to get up. I reminded myself of why I was doing all this. How I wanted to walk again and regain some kind of normality. That's why I was doing all this and that's why I needed to keep going. If the physio is not working, then let's find a different path that will lead to the same goal.

GOLDEN NUGGET

'If the path doesn't lead you to your goal, change the path but never the goal.'
– Steve Judge

The decision to ask for help from my surgeon led to a highly complex operation. They fitted an additional cage to the top of my leg with metal rods that connected to the bottom cage. I woke up from the operation screaming. Pulses of pain jerked through my body with the new metalwork that surrounded the whole of my leg like some sort of scaffolding.

Eventually my screams were suppressed with morphine and over the next 24 hours the task at hand became clear. It was my responsibility (with small spanners) to twist the nuts and bolts in order to gradually straighten my leg. There were no restrictions to the speed of the task apart from the excruciating pain that I would have to subject myself to and live with through the days and the sleepless nights. I was back in the wheelchair and my independence was diminished for those seven weeks of hell. Having the foresight, understanding and knowledge of my golden soul as to why I was subjecting myself to this pain encouraged me to keep going, turn by turn, day by day, week by week until this particular task was complete on my journey towards my GOLD.

· What's your why?

This is a well-known question that the author and inspirational speaker Simon Sinek asks in his bestselling book *Start with Why* (2009). But why do you need to know your why? Maybe you've had a similar question going around your head. Maybe you've had conversations with members of your team or with colleagues:

- Why should I get out of bed?
- Why should I go to work?
- Do I have to eat healthily?
- Why are we still pushing forward on the project?
- Do I have to make an effort this evening?

Engaging you, your team or your employees to tune into the emotional state of their golden soul is an important part of keeping the energy and motivation going. In my workshops and coaching sessions there are five initial questions that I ask to dig down into why the delegates want the thing that they truly want. I call these questions my '5 GOLD things' (you can sing that phrase if you want to!).

5 GOLD things

1. What will you see, feel, hear, etc, when you have it?
2. How will you know when you have it or achieve it?
3. What will the outcome allow you to do, or what will it get you?
4. What will you lose if you achieve it? (This might seem like a strange question but you may lose something bad, which is a good thing, right? On the flip side you may lose something good, such as time with your family.)
5. What will you gain when you achieve it?

My golden soul through rehabilitation

My overall aim after the accident was to stand again, walk again and get back to normal. (I later discovered that there is no such thing as normal but that's a different story.) With all big goals you have to break them down into bite-sized chunks. I just wanted a straight leg. This is what I needed to consider when I was finding my golden soul. Answering the questions in the 5 GOLD things exercise made me aware of and understand the build-up of motivation that was in my head, heart and soul.

What will you see, feel, hear, etc, when you have it?
I will see my leg straight to the point where I can lock it out, stand and bear weight on it. This will enable me to walk freely outside and feel the fresh air.

How will you know when you have it or achieve it?
When the protractor reading results equal 180 degrees and when I can stand on my leg without it buckling.

What will the outcome allow you to do, or what will it get you?
The outcome of a straight leg will allow me to stand up straight without my bum sticking out. I will be able to bear weight fully through my right leg, which will then enable me to walk with reciprocating gait movement. This will take me closer to normality as I'll move closer to independence.

What will you lose if you achieve it?
As I will be able to put full weight through my leg, the bone will grow back strong and that will mean that I can get rid of this damn metal cage round my leg. I will lose the pain that it causes and the discomfort. I will lose the stares from onlookers and the constant questions I get asked about what I've done to my leg.

What will you gain when you achieve it?
I will gain the ability to do more with my leg, to walk, cycle and swim without dragging a cage through the swimming pool. I will gain the accolade of achievement as I work through this challenging period of rehabilitation.

As I answer the questions, it builds up a vision in my mind of what I want and just as importantly why I want it. My brain starts to believe it and conceive it and I'm energised to start taking action to work towards it and achieve it.

Motivating myself in this way brings out the excitement and the passion of my future GOLD. This does, however, leave out the small detail of how on earth I'm going to actually achieve it, but I'll cover this in the next chapter.

GOLDEN NUGGET
'People often say that motivation doesn't last. Well, neither does bathing – that's why we recommend it daily.'
– Zig Ziglar

Habits and miracle routines

It's funny how, no matter how amazing the end goal may be, the journey towards it can be full of trials, tribulations and excuses. Some, believe it or not, we create ourselves or make up and then justify!

Me: 'Hmmm, I was going to go for a run tonight but now it's raining.'

Me: 'So put a coat on and get yourself out there. Don't lean on your excuses, Steve!'

Me: 'That's a good point but I don't want to make myself ill, do I? I think I should stay in and keep warm for the sake of my health.'

Me: 'Really?'

Finding your golden soul is paramount to moving towards your GOLD but you will need more than just that to keep going. There are lots of tools that I use every day to keep me motivated, energised, committed and dedicated. James Clear has written an amazing book called *Atomic Habits* (2018).

Briefly, it's about how making micro changes in your life and building up routines and habits can progress you forward to achieve spectacular results and life-altering outcomes. As a speaker I once shared the stage with James and I listened to his performance from the sidelines and loved it. I was nodding in agreement with his wise words. 'Yep, I do that, yep, I do that too and yep, I also do that.'

But every now and again I would say, 'Ooh, I don't do that; that's a good one. I'm going to start doing that.' We can all keep learning and absorbing new tools and techniques that will help us to achieve. Some will work and some will not because everybody's different but we have to at least try them to find out.

James lays out four laws of behaviour change that are so simple, even I can do them (and that means you can, too):

- How can I make it obvious?
- How can I make it attractive?
- How can I make it easy?
- How can I make it satisfying?

James obviously expands on these laws and goes into a lot more detail in his book, which I highly recommend. While I'm on the subject of recommending books let me suggest another which synchronises beautifully with James's – Hal Elrod and his amazing book *The Miracle Morning* (2012).

The clue is in the title and although I already had a morning routine, this book really helped me to understand the importance of having one and how to embed it fully. When time is tight and you're looking for any spare minute or hour that you can salvage throughout your busy day I found that the morning held a secret stash. It wasn't a lot of time but it was 'my time' and I needed to use it to the best of my ability.

> **GOLDEN NUGGET**
> *'I want to live my life in such a way that when I get out of bed in the morning, the devil says, "Aw shit, he's up!"'*
> – Steve Maraboli

Now is the winter of our discontent

As an elite athlete I had two alarms on my watch, one at 5.30 am and the other at 10.30 pm. The first was 'my time' when I would get up in order to squeeze in an early morning swim session before I started work at 8.30 am. Consequently the 10.30 pm alarm was set because I realised early on that I needed to consistently get to sleep at a reasonable time so that I could get up and work towards my GOLD. My wake-up tune was 'One Vision' by Queen. The lyrics ignited my golden soul, waking up my energy and enhancing my focus. One body, one fire, one passion and one ambition for me to proceed on my journey to become a world champion. This was my routine and my habit as I silently and efficiently changed into the clothes I'd laid out the night before and grabbed my pre-packed swim bag and work bag. Opening the fridge, I'd take out the breakfast, lunch and energy drinks that I had prepared the evening before. 'Grab and go, don't be slow,' I muttered to myself as time is precious.

Winters were the hardest. It was dark, cold and at that time in the morning an eerie silence echoed around the streets where I lived, telling me that the world was still asleep. There were no birds singing, there was no glimmer of a sunrise, the world was still tucked up in bed, cosy and warm apart from me.

Diving to destiny

Sometimes I cycled and other times I drove through the blackness, with the rain and sleet splashing against the windscreen trying to blur my vision as I continued towards my destination at the Sheffield leisure complex Ponds Forge. I moved through reception and the changing rooms on automatic pilot as the anticipation of a rigorous swim session pumped adrenaline through my body in preparation. Standing at the side of the pool I always gritted my teeth before I dived in. Why? I'll tell you why: because it was freezing! Sorry, I mean it was 'training temperature'.

Let me explain. After a couple of lengths, once your muscles kick in and the blood and adrenaline pump freely through your body, then the water temperature is perfect. Perfect for you to excel and push your body to the max with every stroke, completing every length and every kilometre of the session. But let me tell you, diving in, it was flippin' cold! As I gritted my teeth and approached the pool edge a flash of questions would flood my thoughts. Why are we doing this again? What exactly are we trying to achieve here? Is this really worth it? I knew the answers instantly so I would dive in towards my destiny.

Icy daggers of pain

Cycling was no easier through the winter months as I desperately applied layer after layer of Lycra in a lame attempt to combat the arctic conditions. The ruthless hills of Derbyshire aided my body in building up heat and sweat as I dug in deep on the ascents but the cold air penetrated my body like icy daggers on the descents, especially my hands. I was unaware that I actually suffer from Raynaud's disease, which means that my fingers don't just get cold, they get agonisingly cold. The pain would feel like someone was squeezing the ends of my fingers with pliers. I just thought I needed to 'pull myself together' or wiggle my fingers more to increase blood circulation. I was distraught when on one occasion I had to turn back after 15 minutes because the pain in my fingers was causing me to lose concentration to an unbearable degree and I knew I was going to struggle to complete my training session. On my return home I was unable to enter the house due to the temperature difference and spent a full 10 minutes walking round the garden clenching and unclenching my hands in a vain attempt to pump the blood. The squeezing pain in the tip of my fingers led me to wail in pain with my jaw clenched and tears rolling down my cheeks.

'This is crazy, this is ridiculous. Why am I putting myself through this? Why am I doing this to my body? Why am I subjecting myself to so much pain?'

Again, I knew the answers and after I got some sort of feeling back in my fingers, I proceeded to set up the static turbo trainer in the garage for my bike. Once again I pushed onwards towards my GOLD in a dimly lit, uninspiring, static state. Although the environment was lacking in fulfilment, I was fully motivated as I stared down at the sweat-covered screen of my speedometer. Once again, I used my golden soul to think about what I could do rather than what I couldn't as I pedalled onwards towards my GOLD.

Running with the dead

When it comes to running, I create so much body heat that winter sessions cause fewer problems for me than cycling. However, there are still issues to deal with. One slip on the icy surface causing injury could potentially put me out for a month or two or even a whole season. Track training took place once a week with the Sheffield Triathlon Club at Chaucer School, where it was essential for me to build up my speed and perfect my technique. I remember turning up in the evening in sub-zero temperatures, dressed in so many clothes that I looked like the Michelin man. As the running drills evolved under the stadium lights, one by one I removed my protective layers of clothing, eventually just wearing shorts, a long-sleeved T-shirt, gloves and a hat. But even then, sometimes there were weather conditions that just couldn't be accommodated at the track. Snow or a thin layer of ice covering the track surface caused sessions to be cancelled. In the Scouting movement our motto was always 'Be prepared', so I was ready for a situation such as this. I had a 'Plan B'. After work I would drive up to the Grade II listed Sheffield General Cemetery. The path that circulated the perimeter was an adequate distance and as it was gravel it ensured that the frost and ice did not create such treacherous conditions. I would time myself on specific sprint sessions round the dark and dimly lit graveyard. I was committed to working on my pace, consistency and technique and used the steep gradient for power training. A blizzard would hit my face in an attempt to stop my progress but it failed! Knowing my golden soul empowered me to know what had to be done. I knew why I was doing it and what I was working towards. And most importantly I knew that I wouldn't be beaten.

My golden soul as an elite athlete

At times, I couldn't help but have many questions spinning around in my head, asking myself if I was on the right path and doing the right thing despite the consequences. 'Why am I putting myself through this hell? Is the journey that I'm travelling worth the barriers, obstacles and pitfalls that I'm encountering?' I had to dig deep to find the answers. After pondering the 5 GOLD things, I knew what my answers were. What will I see, feel and hear when

I achieve it? I was working towards becoming champion of the world, representing Great Britain, wearing the GB kit. I knew when I'd achieved my goal because I'd have the gold medal round my neck. It was important to me because surely, at the age of 38, this was a chance in a lifetime. To achieve this status would push me forward on my journey away from the accident. I would distance myself from what had happened to me in an attempt to lose the negativity of it. What will I gain from it? Well, I've always said that the accident hadn't ruined my life, just changed it. This was my chance to change it for the better.

I was told that I may never walk again. Pah! I told myself that I'd never run again. Pah! The winter weather was not going to stop me in my quest. Nothing was going to stop me as I pushed forward with resilience and strength. I would eventually compete against the rest of the world in order to quash the anger and resentment about what had happened to me. I hoped that this quest could give me acceptance and enable me to move forward with peace of mind. That's what I wanted and this was why I was doing it. This was my main focus and this was my opportunity. I was on a challenging journey but my desire to achieve pushed me onwards. Knowing all this deep down in my golden soul helped me through the early mornings, through the harsh winters, and enabled me to smash through the barriers that were placed in front of me on the way to my GOLD.

Sulking Steve

When working in a team, department or business it's important for everyone to know why you're all doing what you're doing. Knowing your own 'why' helps you to stay on the path that you have set for yourself. When you've been knocked down it gives you the reason why you should get up and keep moving forward. Without it you'd be tempted to wallow in self-pity and maybe have some chocolate cake or surf the internet for some funny cat videos to cheer you up. Now, I'm not saying that we don't all need some downtime. This can come in the form of wellness, taking time out and looking after ourselves. Sometimes it's just about giving ourselves time to lick our wounds, contemplate, reflect or even just time to sulk, but it gets to a point when you must have a word with yourself about what's going on.

'Are we still sulking, Steve?'

'Damn right we are... I'm not happy.'

'Fair enough, just thought I'd check. And by the way, just to remind you that no one else is sulking, just you, so when you've finished, maybe we could, you know, move on?'

'Yeah, whatever.'

I know that as usual I'm speaking complete sense to myself. And that's it. Sometimes I may sulk for a bit and other times it's for longer but at the end of the day it's my choice. It's my decision as to when I'll stop sulking, pick myself up and start moving forward.

> **GOLDEN NUGGET**
> *'Fall down seven times, get up eight.'*
> – translated from *Nana korobi, ya oki*, a Japanese proverb

My current golden soul

So where am I now? In a way my frustration is driving me – my frustration about others who are not achieving their potential and are 'flatlining' through life, not seizing opportunities or being the best that they can be. Asking myself the 5 GOLD things helps me to truly know what my golden soul is.

What will you see, feel, hear, etc, when you have it?
I will see people achieving their dream, their desire; they will show me and tell me.

How will you know when you have it or achieve it?
For me this is ongoing. I'll continue to share my story internationally to multiple audiences as well as run my workshops but I'll also be laying down a legacy. I'll do this through my books or elearning workshops or by film or song; who knows? Seeing how these are being used by people for them to achieve their GOLD will give me the satisfaction that I'm achieving what I set out to do.

What will the outcome allow you to do, or what will it get you?
I think it will get me resolution from the accident. Let me explain. People often ask me, 'Are you glad that the accident happened, Steve? You know, with all your medals, accolades and travelling round the world, living the life?' My simple answer to this is 'no'. I nearly died that day and the pain and suffering that my mum, brother, sister and loved ones went through as well as myself is unimaginable. I wish the accident had never happened. I'm in pain every day and it only gets worse. The thing is, I can't change what happened to me. Put it this way, when I've inspired and positively changed enough people in this world, I look forward to saying, 'I'm glad the accident happened; I'm glad I nearly died on that day back in 2002 and I'm glad I'm in pain every day! Because of what happened I've become a positive influence on enough people, so much so that it outweighs the negativity that my friends, family and myself have been through. I look forward to that day.' And you may then ask, 'How many people is that? How many people do I have to help?' And my answer is, 'I don't know yet but I'll know when I know.'

What will you lose if you achieve it?
As I mentioned earlier, I think I'll lose the frustration I have with people who don't know how to achieve their goals. I will have spoken worldwide and put so many tools in place that I will have

made it easy and barely an inconvenience for people to know what their GOLD is and then achieve it.

What will you gain when you achieve it?
For me it's all about living with no regrets – by gaining joy from other people's achievements I'll gain the satisfaction that I couldn't have done any more and therefore I'll have no regrets.

Who is the one and only?

If music be the food of motivation, play on. Reminding myself of my golden soul is a great source of inspiration but I also use music to help me through certain moods. I'm always happy to share my music with others but I also realise that styles of music can be a very personal preference. Don't judge me on my music choices; there's nothing wrong with Chesney Hawkes, Eminem or AC/DC! The beauty of this is that when I'm struggling with motivation all I have to do is reach for my phone, select and press play. The music takes care of the rest of it.

Vision board

I mentioned creating a vision board at the beginning of this chapter. This is another technique that I use. You source images from magazines or printouts from the internet of what your goals and visions are and stick them onto a big sheet of paper or card. It can be for the year ahead or even further. It can be just for you or for you and your partner or for your whole family. Once again you can consider the eight areas from the wheel of life and use them as a guide for what you want to do, achieve or accomplish in the future. This can be a fun and once again a physical activity as you cut out and place images onto your vision board to create your future scenario. Once complete, this should be put up in pride of place where you will see it consciously or subconsciously every day so it reaches out to your RAS and energises you to take action and move towards your GOLD.

> **GOLDEN NUGGET**
> *'Life is never made unbearable by circumstances but only by lack of meaning and purpose.'*
> – Viktor Frankl, *Man's Search for Meaning*

Get a proper job?

In my business I use my golden soul as part of my vision and mission and for anybody who's been to a networking meeting, I abbreviate it to form my 'elevator pitch'. But it's when I'm truly tested that I use it to justify why on earth I'm doing what I'm doing and why I'm pushing myself through challenging times. When it comes to challenges with regard to my business, I don't think they can get any bigger than the Covid-19 pandemic. As a conference speaker there certainly weren't many conferences taking place and although I diversified into online keynotes, workshops and coaching, the one thing that I truly loved had been stolen from me. This is not what I'd signed up for! I wanted to be on stage in front of a live audience, inspiring and empowering people. I wanted to hear their gasps, feel their emotions and hear their laughter. Having the crowd on mute or even with videos turned off was demoralising and I longed to get back to in-person events. The lack of work also had an impact on my income and things were certainly tight.

It was during this time at a socially distanced gathering that one of my friends asked me how I was doing through these challenging times. I always openly joke that my job is not a proper job but I like it that way. This time, however, there wasn't that much to laugh about. My friend politely suggested to me whether or not I'd consider putting my business to one side and instead find a different job. I guess they were edging me towards one of those 'proper jobs' – maybe as a team support manager or even helping out at vaccine stations or supermarkets, somewhere that would give me stability and a steady stream of income. I politely declined the suggestion and promptly changed the conversation but I couldn't get what they'd said out of my head and I buried it deep down.

I didn't sleep well that night and the next day, my alarm went off as usual at 5.30 am. I automatically started my golden morning routine of reading for personal development, journaling, visualisation, words of affirmation and floor exercises before I went downstairs to carry out my session on the rowing machine. It was during this lull in my routine when the words from the previous evening circulated in my head, twisting and turning my thoughts and feelings and shaking my emotions. I think we all experienced the corona-coaster of emotions and this onslaught brought a welling of tears to my eyes.

Times in the pandemic were crazy enough for most of us with regard to our mental health and sometimes it just took the slightest crack in the dam to open the floods. As the tears rolled down my cheeks, I had a barrage of emotions flooding my system but the main one was anger. Yes, things in my business were difficult and money was tight. Speaking opportunities were like gold dust and most of my time was spent on lead generation and reaching out to old clients. Times were tough but at no point did I consider quitting. No, I would not give in, and no, I would not go and find a 'proper job'. My golden soul told me what I needed to do. I needed to work harder, be more efficient, be smarter. I needed to keep my health and wellness in check and think about how I could survive in my business and what more I could do to continue on the journey that I had laid down in front of me. I had to keep asking myself how I could keep moving towards the picture that I had drawn on my vision board. Quitting wasn't an option.

> **GOLDEN NUGGET**
> *'When you think of quitting, remember why you started!'*
> – John Di Lemme

Exercise 6: what's *your* golden soul?

Now it's over to you. This exercise is for you to complete immediately. Choose one aspect of your GOLD from the picture that you drew and answer the 5 GOLD things questions to truly find your golden soul. Are you ready? Go for it.

5 GOLD Things

FOCAL POINT

....

What specifically do you want?

....

Where are you now in relation to this goal?

....

1. What will you see, feel, hear etc when you have it?

....

2. How will you know when you have it/achieve it?

....

3. What will the outcome allow you to do, or what will it get you?

....

4. What will you lose if you achieve it?

....

5. What will you gain if you achieve it?

....

Chapter 5

Your golden gear

Until now, I've concentrated on where you are, what you want and why you want it. These aspects relate to yourself or the individuals who make up a team, department or business. They form a solid foundation for what comes next because up to this point, I haven't even mentioned how on earth you're going to move forward on your journey and achieve your GOLD. It has been blue sky thinking with little mention of what obstacles you might actually face on your journey. This is because in my experience just the thought of obstacles allows people to use them as excuses to not even start on the expedition.

As you face the mountain in front of you, you need to consider what gear will help you to conquer it step by step. This is what I call your 'golden gear'. Now comes the time to start planning what you need to do as well as what you need to have both physically and mentally to enable you to succeed. Now is the time to step back from the job at hand, roll up your sleeves and ask yourself, 'Right, how on earth do I tackle this?'

I find that a good way of working out what I need to do at

the start is by remembering what outcome I'm looking for at the end and working backwards to find the steps needed to get there. In my engineering days we would use the term 'reverse engineering', which had been explained to me when I was at college in Doncaster, studying for my Higher National Certificate in Mechanical Engineering.

I knew what I wanted; I just had to work out how on earth I was going to get there. To do this I repeatedly asked myself the question: 'What more can I do?'

Statically moving towards my GOLD

Going through my rehabilitation I was constantly asking myself or others around me, including the surgeons and physios, what other things I could be doing to enhance my progress. In my own personal hospital notes folder, I created a mind map, otherwise known as a spider diagram, where I wrote down all the things that I was doing as well as what I needed to do and also what I wanted to do to further my rehabilitation. I was using my engineering experience and creativity to design and make adjustments to my shoes to improve my mobility. I was having acupuncture on my left leg to see if I could bring some life and feeling back into it. It didn't work but at least I'd tried and therefore I had no regrets. At one point I was doing more than 20 different physio exercises and still I was asking, 'Is there anything else I can do?'

For me, this was my life, this was my priority and I needed to do anything and everything. I was hungry to succeed and although my leg lengthening had gone OK, I was now conscious that growing back my leg bone was the new priority; that was my GOLD. I was bored and impatient with the physio. I wanted something more cardiovascular that would get my heart racing and adrenaline pumping. I was also desperate to do some form of exercise that would pump the blood round my legs as this was important for circulation purposes and to encourage my bone to grow back strong and regain full movement and functionality. I needed to use it, move it and exercise it. I was clearly limited in what I could do as I had a heavy cage on my leg but one day, I had an idea. On my next trip to the hospital, I asked my physio if I could use one of the static exercise bikes that they had in the rehabilitation gym. I explained that I could just sit on the saddle and pedal for a while just to get some movement going.

'Of course not, Steve,' she said. 'Every time your leg goes round, the external fixture will clash with the frame of the bike.' I thought about it and cringed at the concept of my cage smashing into the bike frame. 'Good point,' I said, wincing. 'Fair enough.' I shrugged my shoulders but later on, at home in my wheelchair, I felt differently.

GOLDEN NUGGET

'If you really want to do something, you'll find a way. If you don't, you'll find an excuse.'
– Jim Rohn

I was staring at the exercise bike that I had at home and felt angry inside that this situation was stopping me from progressing towards my GOLD and I was being held back from satisfying my golden soul. The engineer inside me said, 'There must be a way; there must be something that I can do.' I promptly grabbed a pen and wrote on my mind map, 'Cycle on exercise bike'. Then I thought long and hard about how on earth I was going to do that. I reverse engineered the problem by repeatedly asking myself, 'What more can I do?'

The gears in my brain whirred and clunked as an ingenious idea formed. Using my wheelchair and crutches I took myself out to my garage and over a one-day period I actively set about designing and making something that would enable me to satisfy my needs. I was independently using my skills and the euphoria helped me push myself as I was actively working towards my goal. Just as I'm sure Tony Stark felt in the first *Iron Man* film when he was stuck in that cave, using his engineering skills to plan his escape.

Well, my finished project wasn't quite as impressive as an Iron Man suit but what I had produced was a big wooden pedal. It had support brackets and a Velcro strap for my foot and an adjustable nylon strap for fixing it to the bike. I'd even rounded the corners off and smoothed them down. I must admit I was pleased with the craftsmanship. Once an engineer, always an engineer. Bringing it into the house I fixed it onto the pedal and enthusiastically climbed onto the bike, securing my foot in the straps. I started to move the crank. Slowly lifting my knees and pushing them down, I was building up my momentum into a rhythm. Sitting tall on the bike and with the adrenaline pumping, I went faster until endorphins were released. I stared down at my legs. 'Wow... look at me... look at what I'm doing.' I caught myself in the moment and acknowledged my achievement as I was smiling for the first time in a long time. 'I did it!' I said through gritted teeth. 'When others said that I couldn't, I did it.' I had found a way.

I told myself that in future, when someone tells me that I can't do something or even if I tell myself that I can't do something, I must ask myself, 'Is that a fact or an excuse?' If it's a fact, then fair enough. But if it's an excuse then I've got to turn it round. I've got to make sure that I don't lean on my excuses and instead turn my excuses into challenges.

Producing the podium project plan

Following my success in the paratriathlon British Championships, I was thrust into a steep learning curve into the world of triathlon. I felt that I was on catch-up in terms of all the things that I should already be doing as an elite athlete. My source of knowledge initially came from the Sheffield Triathlon Club, combined with books, triathlon magazines and the internet. Being accepted onto the GB paratriathlon squad enabled me to attend the training camps at Loughborough University. These events presented a smorgasbord of facilities, practitioners and a huge number of training techniques. With eyes wide, I acknowledged all that was on offer to help me achieve my GOLD.

Around this time, I came across a cartoon image drawn by Guy Downes showing winners on top of a podium built from many bricks, each labelled with something like 'desire', 'focus' and 'hard work'. It portrays what people don't see with regard to high achievers as well as showing what they have been through to succeed in their quest or challenge.

This image signified to me where ignorant comments come from such as:

'It's alright for you.'

'You're so lucky.'

'You've got it easy.'

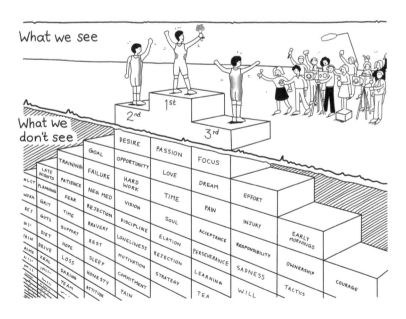

I realised that some people will never fully understand what it's taken to get where I am and never will with regard to what I'll achieve in the future. The time, commitment, dedication, sacrifices, failures and learnings – all of these have enabled me to move forward in my journey towards achieving my goals. But for me to reach that height of achievement, in all cases I've had to reverse engineer the whole concept.

I saw this cartoon image and visualised myself on the podium, mindful of all the elements below of what I needed to do to get there. The gears in my head started whirring and I promptly grabbed a pen and a large sheet of paper and made my own 'podium project plan' template. In reference to the golden vision that I had drawn, I was now standing in celebration on the podium. The key to my success was the blocks I had climbed up on to get me there. I took inspiration from some of the categories in the cartoon image, such as strategy, effort and courage. I didn't like the block that said 'fail' but I guessed that if I could fail fast then I could move on and upwards.

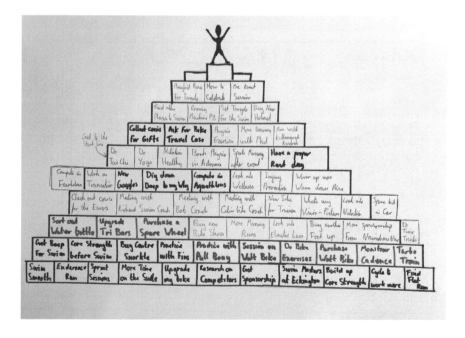

I'd already sorted out some of the blocks, such as my training coaches and some of my gear and equipment. This supplied a necessary and steady foundation but, like I've already said, I was hungry for more.

What more can I do?

What more can I do?

What more can I do?

At the training camp there were sessions about nutrition, strength and conditioning as well as mindfulness and personal development. As I gathered more information, spoke to more athletes and practitioners and considered various possibilities, I found myself filling in more of the blocks on my podium project template. This was great – this was the stuff that I needed, the 'golden gear' that I required. Combined with my hard work, drive and dedication, these tools would take me towards my dream, my GOLD of becoming a world champion. But little did I know that sometimes it's what I didn't need rather than what I did need that would help me on my journey.

Less is more

I discovered that it wasn't always about doing more; sometimes it was just as important to do less. What I mean is that I realised I had to do less of one thing but more of something else. As the months went by, I was getting to some of the start lines of my triathlons and realising that my friends, colleagues and competitive teammates weren't there. I would ask 'Where's Andrew, where's Jasper?' and the short answer was 'They're injured.'

My heart sank for them, as I knew how important this race was to them and how much time and dedication they had put into their training and preparation. I was gutted for them and it struck me that I didn't ever want to be in the situation that they were in now. My neg med was going crazy! I decided that if I didn't ever want to be in that position I had to do something about it.

What more can I do?

What more can I do?

What more can I do?

I think with most things I'm tempted to push hard and push through. You know, dig deep and push through the pain, work longer hours, burn the candle at both ends. But because it was long term, I had to take a step back and weigh it all up. I had to start listening to my body more and start taking action. I had to do the whole 'injury prevention' thing, which between you and me is boring as hell but totally necessary so I amended my podium project plan with preventative aspects.

GOLDEN NUGGET

'Wellness is about taking action so that you can take action.'
– Steve Judge

I had to start concentrating on warming up before and after exercising for up to 10–15 minutes at the side of the pool before I could dive in or in my garden before I got on my bike or set off on a run. Even when I was completely shattered and just wanted to collapse, I completed a cooling down session after the exercise. My strength and conditioning sessions now incorporated flexibility exercises, ensuring that I was focused on taking care of my body.

I needed to give myself some downtime, which as an elite athlete is so hard because I just wanted to push myself and become stronger and faster without resting. I started thinking more about my nutrition, listening to my body and improving my mindset. I ensured that I gave myself time to do some meditation and visualisation so that I could truly focus on what I wanted and make sure that my mind, body and soul were in the right place to achieve. I introduced yoga and tai chi into my routine and daily habits. I was writing down so much on my podium project sheet and implementing it so that I could keep going and be the best that I could be. I'd book physio sessions when I wasn't injured as a preventative maintenance routine. This eradicated the panicked phone calls to my physio, such as, 'Help, I'm injured and I've got the European Championships in two weeks' time! Can you fix me?'

The hardest thing about all this is that you don't necessarily see any results. Instead, you just don't get injured and that in itself is the result. I can happily say that after all these efforts, it worked. I had a few ongoing niggles throughout my career as an elite athlete and even a few minor injuries but nothing that stopped me from competing. No major injuries or wellness issues ever stopped my progress or prevented me from getting to the start line. And I smile when I state that because it's so important. In today's busy world of personal and professional multi-tasking, we're constantly on the go. Getting to your start line is crucial. If you can't do that, then you can't work towards your GOLD and achieve it.

GOLDEN NUGGET
'If you can't get to the start line you can't even compete.'
– Steve Judge

A tasty tool to triumph

Another tool that we were encouraged to use at the GB training camp was the SMART tool (see below). It was explained to all the athletes that it's not always through lack of effort that people don't achieve goals – it's more often due to their lack of clarity. Vague goals such as 'I want to have a better swimming technique' or 'I need to cycle more on my bike' don't work. They need to be specific.

It's the same in the business world. If your goals are 'We want better employee retention' or 'We want our sales to increase' they're not specific enough. What exactly does 'better' mean? 'Increase' by how much? And when does this have to happen?

Being able to view all the blocks and the elements that would take me to my GOLD, I was now able to prioritise the ones that were most important, that needed to be completed first, which were generally the ones at the base of the podium as these form a foundation.

SMART is a tool that you can use to guide your goal setting, originated by George T. Doran (1981). The acronym stands for:

- Specific
- Measurable
- Achievable
- Results desired
- Time based.

There are many discussions and disputes about what the 'R' stands for. I like 'results desired' but some say that 'relevant' makes more sense while others say 'realistic'. I'm sure there are a few other variations, so use whatever works for you. The fact is that most people agree that using SMART goals is a great stepping stone system to work towards your big goal. But there's more!

With the amalgamation of two of my strategies – your golden vision and your golden soul – the SMART acronym extends to SMARTIE, where the 'I' stands for inspiring and the 'E' stands for emotional. It's a tasty way of working towards your triumphs.

The inspiring and emotional elements will help you to keep going on your journey even when you feel like leaning on your excuses. If you refer back to the inspiring golden vision that you drew, you should be able to make the connection to how this specific goal will help you understand the big picture and what you're working towards. To get specific inspiration for this precise goal, I'd advise you to draw another picture of what you're working towards or at least do some visualisation. Focus on what you want to achieve and how the outcome will inspire you to keep going. For emotion, refer back to Chapter 4: you can once again use the 5 GOLD things to question yourself on this particular part of the journey. It will help you to appreciate and fully understand the real reason why you are working on this specific goal. Remember that finding your emotion will create energy and motion.

I kept referring back to my athlete podium project plan, especially the priority goals, and then created a SMARTIE goal setting sheet for each one. It took some time but it really brought each of the goals to life and made it clear what exactly was going to be achieved, why, when and also what action had to be taken for me to reach the podium.

With the positive experience I'd had with my wellness and how I'd been proactive rather than reactive, I amended the SMARTIE sheet to include this. This section was also encouraged through my neg med sessions. I inserted a section that prompted me to think about possible obstacles – things that I thought might stop me or hinder me. For example, as an athlete my greatest fear was injury, but there were other factors such as finding time for training or funding or diary clashes with other important events. The section adjacent to this was 'possible solutions' where I could brainstorm ideas and actions that in a perfect world would ensure that the barrier or obstacle would never manifest or hinder my progress. If funding was going to be a problem further down the line, then I needed to start looking for sponsorship. Consequently, another block would be inserted onto my podium project plan and another SMARTIE goal created. Not all potential obstacles are easy to resolve, which is why you sometimes need a helping hand or input from others. These will be members of your golden gang – and this will be covered in the next chapter.

Exercise 7: the SMARTIE sheet

Opposite is the SMARTIE template for you to use when planning out your individual goals. Remember, this is not for every single block on your podium project plan but just for the larger, main priority goals that need to be broken down.

Are you ready to be SMART with your goal planning? Maybe treat yourself to some Smarties when you've finished. Over to you.

I use the SMARTIE goal in my business but I'll explain more about that in Chapter 7. I'll share when I use it and how it helps me focus on tasks by month, week, day and hour within the Good to GOLD concept.

Hey Siri, my name's Alexa

Following my retirement as an international athlete, I'd spoken at a few schools and business conferences and I'd even completed a week-long speaking tour of Mexico, which was hugely successful with great accolades. One of my goals for the tour was to present parts of my performance in Spanish. Talk about giving myself challenges! *Los Mexicanos apreciaronel esfuerzo que hice para traducir y aprendersu idioma.* ('The Mexicans appreciated the effort I made to translate and learn their language.')

After I was made redundant from my job as a health and safety inspector in construction, I eventually moved forward with setting up my own business as a professional speaker. It's a strange business to get into and one that's hard to explain to others in terms of exactly what I do. When my Cub Scouts, who are aged between eight and ten, ask me what I do for a living, I tell them that I'm a professional speaker. They look at me blankly and say, 'You mean like Alexa or Siri?' Anyway, I knew from my experience that if I wanted something enough then I

SMARTIE Goal Planning Sheet

Priority (1-5) _____ Today's Date _____ Target Date _____ Date Achieved _____

What do you want to achieve?
Specific
Measurable
Achievable
Result desired
Time based
Inspiring
Emotional
So... SMARTIE goal is:

Benefits of achieving this goal (impact on my life/business)

Turn your excuses into challenges

Barriers/Excuses	Consequences	Solution

knew how to get it. I had a vision and I was already focusing on what I wanted to achieve and why I wanted it so much. On a big sheet of paper, I drew the blocks leading up to the podium at the top. On this particular sheet, instead of a podium image, I drew myself on a big stage running my successful business as a professional speaker.

The blocks were filled in with things such as getting a website and business cards as well as networking and, of course, a nice snazzy logo. Within the blocks I knew that I had to start working on my personal development, reading books, attending training courses and growing as a speaker. Then I completed one of my 'podium project' blocks that stated 'Perform at a TEDx speaking event'.

TEDx is an international showcase for speakers who present well-formed ideas in less than 18 minutes. More importantly, apart from the audience of a couple of hundred people, it's also filmed and then shared on the internet for everybody to view, in perpetuity. Setting that as a goal and working towards it led me to speak at the Sheffield Hallam TEDx event in 2015. It was absolutely amazing and really pushed me to up my game.

Following my performance, it was suggested by one of the organisers that I should check out the PSA (Professional Speaking Association). They hold monthly events around the UK where professional speakers go to 'speak more and speak better', share their knowledge and wisdom and encourage others to do the same. This was ideal for me. I found the closest one was PSA Yorkshire, so I booked myself onto the next event in Leeds. After my first visit, I was buzzing. Regional president Emma Sutton asked me if I'd enjoyed it. 'It's been great,' I said. 'The speakers were amazing and the learnings and takeaways were so useful. For me just being in a room full of professional speakers who were "doing it" and running a business through it was all so inspiring for me.' Emma said, 'Wow. Well, if you're interested in becoming a member, you can also enter Speaker Factor.' So I said, 'Speaker Factor? What's that?'

Emma briefly described the annual competition where speakers have five minutes to deliver a talk to an audience. It's a strict five-minute duration – any longer and you get marked down! You're not allowed to use slides and you're judged on your stagecraft, script, delivery and bookability. If you get through the regional heat, you go onto the semi-finals and if you get through that then you're in the final. Only five speakers from around the UK and Ireland get to the finals, where they present at the annual conference in front of more than 200 of the top speakers. I was shaking with nerves and excitement as I was absorbing everything that Emma was saying. 'Wow,' I said. 'It all sounds quite horrific and way out of my comfort zone. Count me in!'

I knew by now that if I ever wanted to achieve anything big in my life, I was going to have to push myself a little bit further than normal. And as I'm sure you're aware, I am a little bit competitive. My goal was to get to the finals and be on that stage in front of that audience of professional speakers in my first year as a speaker. That night I created a separate podium project plan and started filling in the blocks that would take me to the finals of Speaker Factor and onto that main stage.

I promptly joined the PSA, signed up for the competition and started crafting my speech with help from Emma, who initially coached me leading up to the regional heats. I soon learned that it was about a lot more than just having a good story and a lot of confidence. The blocks on my sheet included items such as 'learn about stagecraft' and 'watch videos on delivery techniques'. What does 'bookability' even mean? There was so much to learn about this skill, this new art. I inserted numerous blocks on my page about rehearsals and took action. I rehearsed in front of the wall, in front of the mirror, in front of Emma, in front of the cat, in front of the kids and in front of my partner, Jo. All the time I was asking them for feedback but also asking myself:

What more can I do?

What more can I do?

What more can I do?

I felt good and ready for the Yorkshire regional heat and performed to the best of my ability. Then the results came in… I'd failed as I hadn't won. I couldn't believe it – I was gutted. My vision of getting to the semi-finals, let alone the finals, was gone. The PSA members were so supportive and one after the other they came over to me.

'Steve, that was great, really good. If you want some feedback just let me know.'

'Brilliant work, Steve. What an amazing story. I made some notes for improvement so give me a shout if you want me to help you.'

'Loved it, Steve – just a few adjustments needed but a great presentation.'

They were all saying similar things but I thought, 'What's the point? I've done my best; I'm out of the competition now.' But I wasn't!

It was whispered to me that there was a loophole and I could register in another region and grab a second chance. I felt a surge of adrenaline and excitement, which eradicated my disappointment at not winning. 'A second chance,' I thought, and from that I went from a phase 1 level of feedback up to a phase 4. Let me explain.

Four phases of feedback

'Can I give you some feedback?' That question can send a shiver of discomfort down your spine in many situations. It may be about your clothes or the last board report or even your communication skills. To be fully open to feedback and take action as a result, you need to move from phase 1, which is denial and defensiveness to phase 4 where you are more open to accept ideas and input. The sooner you can make this move, the better.

Phase 1:   F you (Get lost!).

Phase 2:   F you, but I'm listening.

Phase 3:   I'll listen to your feedback but I'm not going to do anything about it.

Phase 4:   I'll take your feedback on board and might consider making some changes.

I've learned that if the suggestions are coming from someone that I know, trust and respect then they are clearly expressing their opinion to help and support me. Listening to and taking on board comments from the PSA members made me realise that my initial reaction to failure was wrong. Instead, the result gave me a prime opportunity to receive valuable feedback and improve.

GOLDEN NUGGET

'There is no failure, only feedback.'

– Robert Allen

I amended my podium project plan with additions such as:

- feedback – phase 4
- register with another PSA region
- amend script
- adjust performance
- rehearse
- rehearse

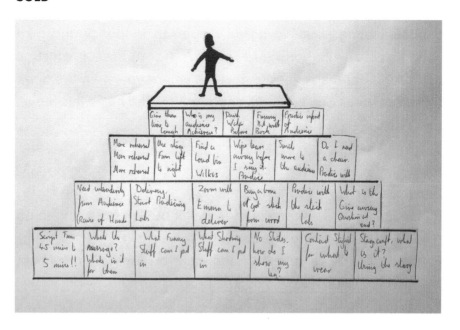

Over the next three months I worked on my delivery and stagecraft with my props, using the stage and interacting with my imaginary audience. I sounded out the emphasis of words and phrases and spoke from the heart because that's when people truly hear you and feel your passion. I adjusted and perfected my script word by word until it flowed and sang out the message that I wanted it to deliver. Like a training montage from the film *Rocky*, I practised, rehearsed and repeated my talk over and over again.

Finally, the date arrived for me to travel up to Newcastle where I competed at the PSA North East Speaker Factor event to the absolute best of my ability. And this time, I won. People said, 'That was incredible. Truly fantastic.' The accolades were great to hear and all the time and commitment I had put in had been worth it – but I wasn't finished. Don't forget I was now at phase 4 for feedback. 'Can you suggest any improvements?' I enquired. 'Is there anything you feel I could work on? What more can I do?'

I'd realised how crucial this feedback was as the next event was the semi-finals against nine other top speakers. I collected all the feedback from the experienced and knowledgeable speakers that I trusted. I carried on improving and perfecting, bit by bit, performance by performance. I got through the semi-finals to become one of the five Speaker Factor finalists. To be there on the main stage in front of more than 200 of the top speakers in UK and Ireland in my first year was an incredible accomplishment. On that day I came a close second to the winner but I was happy. I was happy that I'd done everything and anything that I could do to get that result and because of that I had no regrets. I'd learned so much about the skills and craft of a professional speaker and I was aware that this was just the beginning. My podium project plan had worked by giving me a visual structure and clearly laying out all the aspects that I needed to complete to achieve my goal.

My speaker journey continues

My GOLD is to become one of the greatest speakers in the UK and this encourages me to stay at the phase 4 level of feedback for every performance I deliver and event that I attend. Speaking on the main stage at the Global Speakers Summit in 2022 was an incredible honour and accolade to my position and yet I was still not content. Taking input from the audience, clients, fellow speakers and trusted colleagues, I totally embrace the quote that there is no such thing as failure, only feedback. As a business owner and professional speaker, I'm constantly asking the people around me but more to myself:

What more can I do?

What more can I do?

What more can I do?

What more can YOU do?

Now it's time for you to create your own podium project plan and start considering every single thing that you need to do to work towards your own GOLD. Start filling in each of the blocks from the bottom up by asking yourself those three repetitive questions:

What more can I do?

What more can I do?

What more can I do?

Exercise 8: your podium project plan

The podium project plan exercise is here for you to complete right now.

If you run out of boxes, then download and print off another sheet or maybe enlarge it to a bigger sheet. Be open and creative and let your ideas flow.

There may well be times when you've run out of ideas on how to progress and what new blocks you can insert into your plan. There may be times when you can't think of any obstacles that may get in your way or if you can then maybe you can't think of any solutions to those obstacles. If these are personal goals, then maybe ask your friends or your peers. In work situations you can ask your colleagues or the whole team or department. Maybe form a mastermind group with certain practitioners who fully understand your goals and your drive and can assist in specific ways. They may be able to help through knowledge, experience, expertise or accountability. Whether personal or professional, this motley crew of practitioners, specialists and experts in their field are your golden gang and they will play a vital part in the completion and success of your journey.

Chapter 6
Your golden gang

Working towards your GOLD can be a long journey and no doubt there will be new experiences along the way and new learnings that you'll have to take on board and deal with. The sooner you realise that you need help, the better. This may mean that you have to do that whole 'asking for help' thing, which a lot of people aren't very good at. In fact, a lot of people avoid it like the plague and I include myself in that. 'I'm strong, I've got common sense, I'm wise and I'm independent. I don't need to ask for help... I've got this!' Just reading these words that I say to myself makes me shudder. Yes, I am all those things but if for one moment I think that I have all the answers or don't need any other input, feedback or guidance from anyone else then I am very, very much mistaken.

> **GOLDEN NUGGET**
> *'If you think that you have all the answers then you're wrong.'*
> – Steve Judge

However, there are other times when there's absolutely no doubt in your mind that you require help or support or an answer to a question. I don't mean the kind of help that you get from Google, Siri or Alexa. You're out of your comfort zone, you've bitten off more than you can chew, you're in a hole and time is ticking! This is when you need to reach out, shout or even scream at the top of your lungs. This is when you need your 'golden gang' around you. But not just your current gang – you also need a dream team. You need to plan for the future and have your potential golden gang members all mapped out.

The three rings of the golden gang

Through my experiences from wheelchair to world champion and beyond I've found that there are three rings of golden gang members who have enabled me to go from commencement to fulfilment. Throughout my journeys through rehabilitation, being an elite athlete and then a business owner, I've always had a group of people around me to help and support my progress.

Commencement: My first ring of gang members are those that I need to start my specific journey. As I embark on my expeditions, I need a foundation that I can build on. After the accident, this would have been the people that helped me to survive. In the triathlon world it would have been people that helped me with the basic knowledge of the sport and potential competitions. Within business it's the network of business contacts who helped me to establish a presence, get my message out there and generate an income.

Accomplishment: The second ring of members have supported and enabled me to achieve and accomplish my journey. Understanding one another and being aware of what I was attempting to achieve have been paramount in the attainment of my overall GOLD – to stand and walk again, to become a world champion, to successfully run my business in order for me to empower others to achieve.

Fulfilment: The third ring holds the golden gang members that I feel I deserve and aspire to have in my group as I become more successful. These gang members have a level of supremacy and excellence in relation to my GOLD. As an outpatient I had specialised physios dealing with individual areas of my rehabilitation. While training as a paratriathlete I had a mindfulness coach and top bike mechanic preparing me and my equipment to perform at the highest level. And now I have an award-winning business coach who is enabling my business to thrive. In the future, who knows? Maybe I'll need a helicopter pilot to efficiently fly me around to my gigs!

Planning these three rings of gang members has once again helped me to see who is on the journey with me and also who I need on my journey to take me to the next level. By having a clear picture in my mind of who will help, support and empower me to get to where I want to be, my RAS will open up my vision and steer me towards the people who will make it happen. Whether that's connecting with people on LinkedIn or chatting to potential golden gang members at business networking events.

'Oh, so you're a pilot. A helicopter pilot... how interesting. Do you have a business card?'

What about you? Who is already on your team? Who do you need on your team and who will be joining your team in the future due to your hard work?

The ring of commencement

There was no other time in my life when I needed help more than when I nearly lost my life. That's when I shouted out. That's when I screamed at the top of my lungs and, luckily, help was at hand.

'HELP! Help me! Somebody help me!' These are the words I shouted as I was stuck in my car with my legs crushed and my life slowly slipping away. At that time a complete stranger who was walking his dog was abruptly inducted into my golden gang as he phoned the emergency services and told me, 'Don't worry, help is on the way.' From that point onwards my gang increased incrementally with the paramedic first responder, the police and the fire brigade who spent over an hour cutting me free from the car wreckage. Then the ambulance drivers got stuck in as they whizzed me off to hospital. Yes, the two guys who were coincidentally called Steve and Steve. You can imagine the conversation we had in that ambulance.

'OK Steve, we're going to take you to the nearest hospital. Is that OK, Steve?'

'Yes, Steve,' I replied.

Then the other Steve said, 'We're going to drive very fast, Steve. Is that OK, Steve?'

'Yes, Steve,' I responded.

'And very safely. OK, Steve?'

'Yes, Steve.

I liked these Steves. We formed an instant connection and they joined my gang.

As I entered the safety of the NHS system, the first ring of my golden gang expanded to include staff, nurses, surgeons, anaesthetists, consultants and doctors. Through rehabilitation the physios joined as well as the practitioners at the pain clinic. I recognised and appreciated every single member of the gang that were helping me to reach my goals and my ultimate GOLD of standing and walking again. But as my journey continued, my golden gang needed to expand to another ring of members. When situations or complications arose, I would have to take a step back and work out who I needed to assist me in my journey. Using the golden gear method once again I asked myself over and over, at every stage:

What more can I do?

What more can I do?

What more can I do?

Consequently, with the answers to these questions came the next question, which was 'Who can help me?'

Ten months after the accident my left leg still had limited feeling below the knee and a lack of sensitivity that resulted in a drop foot. The consultant explained to me, 'There's not a lot more than we can do, Mr Judge. Your nerve could have been crushed or even severed.' This wasn't a result that I was happy with or would accept at that point, so I wanted an acupuncturist to do their voodoo pin magic on my leg and bring it back to life. This meant that I had to find another member to recruit for the team. With four inches of leg extension on my right leg, my toes had clawed and I was unable to straighten them, resulting in constantly putting weight through my toenails. The pain and discomfort were excruciating. While the NHS physios concentrated on other parts of my body, I wanted a separate physio who would concentrate on wrenching the hell out of my toes to sort them out. I found my new gang member and the pain sessions commenced. In both of these situations I'd established who I wanted on my gang. I searched for them, found them, recruited them and all together we worked towards my GOLD.

Sadly, in both of these scenarios neither worked. My left leg still has a drop foot combined with a lack of sensitivity, movement and feeling, but I have no regrets as I know I tried everything. I eventually changed my focus onto prosthetic shoes and straps to accommodate my disability and of course I found somebody to help me with that. Eventually, the toes on my right foot had to be individually broken and agonisingly fixed straight with metal pins. I have absolutely no regrets about working through my 'Plan A' first with the physio and the pain. I'm also glad that there was a 'Plan B' and of course another surgeon joined the golden gang to administer the operation. Recognising your golden gang members is so important, as is explaining the full journey you are on so that they can be on it with you.

Thank you costs nothing

Explaining my goal to the members of my golden gang seemed unnecessary at the time as it was clear where I was going but I was on a quest to recognise and thank everyone. A box of chocolates and a simple thank you card didn't seem enough. Once again, I needed help and reinforcements in order to deliver a special thank you. I got married three months after the car accident while still in a wheelchair. At the wedding reception I announced that I needed help from the hundred or so guests. A massive homemade thank you card was passed around the tables and people were encouraged to write a quick note to the services, departments, staff and practitioners who had saved my life. The blank sheets of the card came to life with the most beautiful and colourful messages of appreciation and admiration.

Over the next month I photocopied all the comments and

produced a total of 15 separate cards and then delivered them. The reactions were emotional and heartfelt and the cards were hugely appreciated. I remember seeing those cards a year later in some of those departments, hanging up on the reception noticeboard with members of staff still occasionally reading the comments and acknowledging the gratitude.

GOLDEN NUGGET

'Don't let the sun go down without saying thank you to someone and without admitting to yourself that absolutely no one gets this far alone.'
– Stephen King

The ring of accomplishment

I'm sure you can imagine that when you're representing your country at the World Championships you would have a big team behind you – maybe a bit like an A-list celebrity, film star or rock star with an entourage that follows them around and anticipates their every need.

You need the best conditions and the best treatment because you're there to perform to the best of your ability. Well, you may be right in thinking that but it wasn't always the case. It still sends shivers down my spine when I cast my mind back to my hotel room in Beijing, when I nearly bent the rear forks of my bike by forcefully assembling it in the wrong way. It would have meant I was unable to compete in the event and my dreams would have been shattered. We had no bike mechanic for the event, so it was 'each to their own'. Each athlete assembled their own equipment after the long haul flight to China. Even though I got away with that narrow miss in my hotel room, I wasn't so lucky during the actual race when I had a bad mechanical failure on my bike – but that's a story for another time.

We did have a small team supporting us out in Beijing but it was tiny in comparison to the team that we ended up with two years later. The head coach Jonny Riall had a vision and a goal to get the GB squad to the Paralympics in 2016 and to top the medal table. He had to take it from an amateur sport to a professional one in just a couple of years and knew he couldn't do it alone. He was inspired by what the able-bodied national team were doing and clearly motivated by their fantastic results. He had his first ring of commencement and quickly needed his ring of accomplishment members to take it up to the next level. He knew who he wanted on his golden gang, so now he had to find them and do whatever it took to get them on the team.

One vision

Our visions were combined. As an athlete I wanted to win the gold and Jonny wanted the whole team to win, both individually and on the medal table. Each athlete had their own golden gang. I had a swim, bike and running coach as well as an overall triathlon coach from the Sheffield Triathlon Club. I now had a bike mechanic to fine tune the workings of my equipment and a physio to do the same for me.

Jonny searched out and found professionals and practitioners for the performance squad training weekends down at Loughborough University. On these camps it was refreshing to mix with like-minded individuals. We were all driven and committed to our individual goals as well as the overall goal of the paratriathlon squad and Team GB. We encouraged and supported one another as well as having a laugh and swapping stories. Our hardest task was giving ourselves enough downtime so that we could go again on the next session.

Absorbing myself into the world of triathlon made me realise what I needed to do and what plan of action to take. I saw what other athletes were doing with their training schedules and techniques and was inspired and encouraged by them. Everybody's different and even more so when each athlete has different disabilities to deal with and accommodate. This encouraged me to ask more questions and be even more creative and ingenious with my ideas and methods. Could I improve more on my transition by having elasticated laces in my trainers like Tom? Looking at Claire's bike set-up, maybe I could move the position of my water bottle on my bike to reduce wind resistance and make it easier and safer to hydrate during the race?

My route and my journey were forever filling up with ideas of what I needed to do to successfully achieve my GOLD and who I needed to help me get there. At the European and World Championships we had new staff within the GB paratriathlon performance squad, a new entourage, a new golden gang working in unison to take the GB team to GOLD. Imagine a team of professionals, dressed in GB tracksuits, with shades on, walking in slow motion towards you. That was our golden gang.

We had doctors, physios and strength and conditioning experts as well as coaches who were experts in their fields, nutritionists and bike mechanics. With these members Jonny was ready and prepared to take the team to the next level and on to the Paralympics. He'd done it; he'd created an amazing team and I'd say he'd even verged into the next ring, the ring of fulfilment.

Once, at the 2013 World Championships in London, I remember going to lift my heavy kit bag to put it in the team trailer when one of the golden gang members stopped me. 'We've got this, Steve,' they said. 'Can't risk you getting injured. Just jump on the bus with the other athletes.' Things had certainly changed during my time as an elite athlete and the winning results for team GB backed that up.

> **GOLDEN NUGGET**
>
> *'Coming together is a beginning, staying together is progress, and working together is success.'*
> – Henry Ford

The ring of fulfilment

In my business, I have a chart on the wall that lists who I have in my golden gang and also who I want to have. For me to get to where I want to be, my GOLD, then I've already envisioned who's on my team. Everybody's golden gang structure will be different depending on who you are and what your GOLD is. When I mention that I have a stylist, people may think that they belong in my fulfilment ring but for me as a professional speaker, they belong at the core of my business.

Speak before you've spoken

As I mentioned in the previous chapter, I spoke at a TEDx event. I was just starting out as a professional speaker and this was a big deal for me. Well, to be honest, this was a humongous deal for me. This could go viral and be shared all over the world for everybody to see. This could be it. But I had enough to think about with regard to my script, message and performance and my neg med session told me that I needed to sort out what I was going to wear for the gig and move on. I'd heard of such a thing as a stylist but never thought that I'd needed one until now. My session with Harry Purewal taught me not just which colours make me look good and why but also my style. It's fascinating how the most intricate details can create an impression. I've since realised that by wearing the right outfit it enables me to speak before I've even spoken. As I walk into a room or step out onto the stage, people will look me up and down and either consciously or unconsciously judge me. From the shoes that I wear to the colour of my shirt and even the watch and belt buckle that I'm wearing they all give an indication of the type of person I am. So, the question is whether or not I'm giving the right kind of impression for myself and for my message. It also means that I'm sorted, I know what I need to wear and I can put less thought and time into it because I've got bigger things to think about.

This is similar to Steve Jobs of Apple, who famously wore the same outfit of blue jeans and black turtleneck. He could devote his time to the creative projects that he was working on. Barack Obama had the same idea. He was quoted (by Lewis 2012) as saying, 'You'll see I wear only grey or blue suits... I don't want to make decisions about what I'm... wearing. Because I have too many other decisions to make.'

The TEDx event was a huge success and I felt very comfortable in what I was wearing and how I was being seen. I was the best that I could have been leading up to the event and my stage performance was just how I had envisioned it. It was a great event all round and another completed block on my podium project plan, taking me further on my speaker journey.

Quadrants

As I've moved forward in my business as a professional speaker it's become evident that certain members of my gang fit into similar sectors. Harry, my stylist, works nicely along with my tailor Jason of Lord's Custom Tailors, based in Hong Kong. Also in this sector that we could call 'image' is my hairdresser, Jayne, who's just up the road from where I live. Together they give me the confidence in terms of how I want to be seen. This enables me to prioritise my presentation and performance to give the audience the best experience and deliver my message in the most entertaining and memorable way.

Splitting your golden gang into sectors also allows you to

create a whole new area for a different goal. For example, if you wanted to start a business or move from one position in your career to another then you could create new sectors to accommodate the new members who will help you achieve this. A health and fitness goal may not have any direct connection with your other goals but the positions of dietitian, nutritionist, personal trainer and accountability partner can still go on the golden gang layout chart but just in a different sector. Alternatively, you can create a whole new chart if that's easier to do.

> **GOLDEN NUGGET**
> *'If I have seen further, it is by standing on the shoulders of giants.'*
> – Isaac Newton

Future friends

I'm very happy with where I am in my business but I'm nowhere near content. It's the same with my current golden gang members. They're all awesome and they've all helped me to get to where I am now. There's my business coach Rob, my supportive partner Jo, my mastermind team as well as my website designer and accountant – the list goes on. But thinking about who will be on my future golden gang is great fun and a lovely session to run for others on my workshops. I encourage myself to visualise climbing into my chauffeur-driven car to take me to my next speaking gig. I need a driver because I'm a busy guy – or, as I've mentioned before, I may even need a helicopter pilot! I'd love a nutritionist and a chef to prepare my healthy lunch, as I'm always on the go, plus a personal trainer to keep me at peak fitness and my body in check so that I can perform to the best of my ability. Of course, I've not forgotten about the other aspects that I require in my business, such as a search engine optimisation expert, a marketing guru and a personal assistant, but you've got to cover all angles of your vision, right? Building and planning my golden gang is fun and also gets me excited about what is yet to come. Conceive it, believe it and achieve it.

We all stand together

It's important to me that my golden gang understand the journey that we're on together – for them to know what my GOLD is and just as importantly what my golden soul is. They're aware of the golden gear that I need in order for me to reach my vision and they know they're part of the team that will get me there. They all know this individually but I also have a vision that I'd like to share with you, the reader. My vision is to hold an event with all my gang members present, for me to reiterate my vision and my journey and explain where and how each member plays their part in getting me to my GOLD. After all the seriousness, we'd then celebrate past, present and future achievements. It would be special just to have my entire golden gang in one room just to say thank you to them at a personal level. Who knows, if things go well maybe we'll need another place setting for my helicopter pilot as I arrive in style.

GOLDEN NUGGET

'Find a group of people who challenge and inspire you, spend a lot of time with them, and it will change your life.'
– Amy Poehler

Exercise 9: who's in your gang?

Now it's your turn. Be sure to think about the three rings of members: the ring of commencement, the ring of accomplishment and the ring of fulfilment. Gain satisfaction as you appreciate and acknowledge your current members and have fun creating your future members who will take you towards your GOLD. Within a business or corporation, your company organisation chart would be the ideal starting point for the first two rings but now consider the fulfilment section. What dream positions would you like to be advertising for? What consultants or gurus would you like to be visiting your premises? Go on, think freely and be creative.

Here is the golden gang exercise for you to complete.

Three rings of the golden gang

Once you have your gang, how will you ensure that your team or department or all the members of your gang are working towards the same GOLD? How are you informing, inspiring, motivating or where necessary empowering them to continue in unison on the journey? How are you thanking them in the best way possible so that they fully understand what it means to accomplish the fulfilment of true GOLD? Full appreciation from your golden gang is extremely beneficial as they definitely need to be on board for the rolling out of the structured timescale plan with those stipulated deadlines. All of you will be working in unison throughout the years, months, weeks and days, all the way to the final strategy of the golden hour that will enable the achievement of your GOLD.

Chapter 6
Your golden hour

Time is precious; time is delicate and it should be nurtured and looked after. Time should be respected because it is critical – no more so than when time literally means life or death.

One hour to live or die

I'm still in contact with the two Steves that saved my life and one of them, Steve Cook, told me that as paramedics their medical definition of the 'golden hour' is this: the period of time immediately after a traumatic injury, during which there is the highest likelihood that prompt medical and surgical treatment will prevent death (see also Abhilash & Sivanandan 2020). This was the scenario I faced on that Sunday afternoon as my car crashed, bent in half and crushed both of my legs. The clock was now ticking.

One of the biggest killers following a traumatic incident is when, in an attempt at self-preservation, the body goes into shock and starts shutting down. Having a strong 'mind over matter' strategy as well as optimism can play a big part in your survival in situations such as this. Not many people know what their blood type is. Mine is the relatively rare type B+, pronounced 'be positive', which is exactly what helped to prevent me going into shock. After the hour and a half it took to cut me free from the twisted metal and a half-hour mercy dash by the two Steves in the ambulance, I was rushed through accident and emergency and taken straight into surgery. But by this time my golden hour had long expired and I was on borrowed time, clinging onto life with every ounce of energy that I had left in my limp body. The chances of me making it out alive were slim.

Throughout my ordeal, I had a strange relationship with time. As a patient I became impatient. I didn't want to be in hospital, I wanted to have my operations, recover and then go home but sadly it wasn't as easy as that. I was frustrated that I couldn't do something to speed up the process of recovery, even though at this stage the main thing I needed to do was rest. I found that so annoying. Eight months into my rehabilitation, when I'd twisted the bolts on my cage to lengthen my leg to a full 10 cm, I was ecstatic about concluding this ordeal and getting the cage removed. 'So, when will the cage be taken off?' I politely enquired. 'Well, when the bone grows back, Mr Judge,' the surgeon replied. 'It has to bond and harden enough for weight bearing. It could be a minimum of four months.'

'Four months!' I was absolutely gutted and once again my impatience grew.

GOLDEN NUGGET
'Impatience isn't a bad thing, as long as you use it.'
– Steve Judge

Again, I did everything and anything to speed up this process. I discovered that it wasn't just about eating cheese and drinking milk for the calcium, although I did increase both in my diet, just in case. I also took calcium pills, which were huge and really hard to swallow. I swear they were designed for horses, not humans, but again I was willing to try anything. I was also told that by using my leg this would encourage the bone to grow. 'But there's no bone in my leg,' I said. 'Just this cage that is bridging the gap and holding my leg together.' The surgeon replied, 'We understand that Mr Judge. But you need to walk on your leg – trust the cage.' Trust the cage? That's easier said than done.

Using a Zimmer frame, I slowly put weight through my leg. It was one of the most difficult mind games I've ever played, knowing that part of my leg had no actual bone in it. Through gritted teeth and with sweaty palms I complied with the requirements. I eventually moved on to walking round the house on my crutches and then venturing out of my comfort zone even further, going round my housing estate every day, week and month. I used my impatience to drive me forward into growing my bone back and getting the cage removed. Periodically they X-rayed my leg with the same feedback: 'It just needs a bit more time.'

This excerpt is from my rehabilitation notes, written in June 2003, a year after my accident:

Title: How good?
How good do you want to be?
How much time are you willing to give?
Training
Practice
Endurance
Persistence
Commitment
Time
Time, time, time
Give a lot and you will receive
How good do you want to be?

Month after month, X-ray after X-ray, I got the same frustrating answer. I pushed myself even further, going to a local park called Rother Valley, where I had built up to a distance of 5K by walking round the two lakes in order to grow and solidify the bone and ultimately build up its strength. I was literally doing anything and everything to get this cage taken off. I turned my impatience into dedication and commitment to move forward and succeed in what I set out to do.

The day that I got the green light to have the cage removed I was elated. Then I asked if they were sure. There was no way that I wanted to undo all my hard work if there was a possibility that my bone wasn't quite as solid as the X-ray made it out to be and it might break or collapse. They assured me I was good to go.

It had taken a whole year to grow my leg back. Because of my persistence every month, every week, every day and every hour, I had finally achieved my goal. It also meant that at last I was able to wear proper long trousers for the first time since the car accident. Up to this point all my trousers had Velcro sewn in down the seam for easy application over the cage – a bit like the trousers that male strippers wear, so I'm told!

My rehabilitation taught me to appreciate time – the time that I have and how I use it. I was like a caged tiger, locked up for nearly two years, so when the cage was opened, I felt free. It was like an explosion of adrenaline and excitement and a time to explore new opportunities and possibilities. For me it was my second life, almost a new beginning. Possibly I didn't actually see it like that then but looking back I think that description makes a lot of sense. From this experience I learned to live my life with no regrets because I've only got one shot at this thing.

Achievement through the use of time

I'm going to be open and honest here because I believe it's what you deserve from me. I feel that we've built up a nice close relationship as you've been reading this book. I'm not that keen on setting specific deadlines as to when I'm going to achieve something. But the fact is, I know it works. Just using the phrase 'as soon as possible' is not a good enough goal to work towards, especially on big projects. A deadline or specific date is such a driver for me – it's incredible how I can pull out all the stops and make sacrifices to achieve it. Even if it's last minute, it still counts, right?

The best deadlines are the ones that can't be moved. I remember at school when I rushed to hand in homework on time and the teacher had pity on all the students who had failed to deliver and moved the submission date to the following week. It wasn't a good lesson for working towards goals and deadlines in the real world because life is not as forgiving as that.

New kid on the block

In 2012, when I got beaten in the European Championships by four minutes by the Italian Michele Ferrarin, my dream of becoming world champion that year was shattered. He was awesome, especially in the swim, where he swam like a fish. I'd just achieved personal best times in the swim, bike and run to grab the silver medal and with that came the realisation that there was no way I could go any faster – especially four minutes faster for the World Championships in New Zealand in six months' time, no way!

My head was spinning and I was in turmoil. But then my golden vision and my golden soul flashed into my mind, reminding me of why I was doing all this. It made me stop and take a mental step backwards. I suddenly realised that I was looking at this deadline all wrong. I was leaning on my excuses and had to turn my excuses into challenges. I had six months to become four minutes faster. I was doing that whole reverse engineering thing again. I knew what I wanted, my GOLD; I just had to work out how on earth I was going to get there. I thought about my golden vision and reiterated my golden soul to myself. I also needed a refreshed golden gear podium project plan.

What more could I do?

What more could I do?

What more could I do?

I expressed my passion and quest to my golden gang and asked for their help.

> **GOLDEN NUGGET**
> *'We all have time; it's how we cultivate time that determines what we achieve.'*
> – Steve Judge

Going for GOLD

I wanted to win. I wanted to be world champion out in New Zealand and just needed to work out how I was going to achieve it in the time that I had available. My deadline was the finish line. In six months I worked on my swimming technique to become even more efficient and save my energy for the other two disciplines. I committed even more time to my bike training to build up my endurance and increased my strength to become even faster on the run. I was conscious of injury prevention and balanced my time appropriately with my wellness so that I could get to the start line.

Then it was to New Zealand for the World Championships and, yes, Michele Ferrarin was there. The start horn went off and Michele disappeared through the sea like a fish, with me following in his wake. On the bike I couldn't even see him but I was chasing, digging deep and pushing hard. On the run section I was hunting; I needed to see him. Once I could see him, I could catch him and if I could catch him, I knew I could take him. Step by step, I moved closer and closer until I was level with him. I was flying but running on empty. As I overtook him, I continued to focus ahead on what I wanted to achieve rather than looking behind me at what I wanted to avoid. I pushed hard round the final corner and crossed the finish line to be crowned champion of the world for the second year running.

For me this proves that by having a deadline and the right mindset in combination with my Good to GOLD concept, I was able to move mountains, hit that deadline and achieve such an incredible result. How to set those deadlines can be challenging but luckily, in my business, my coach Rob is able to help me.

GOLDEN NUGGET
'A goal without a deadline is just a dream.'
– Robert Herjavec

Turning a vision into a plan

My coach Rob asked me, 'Where's your five-year plan, Steve?' I said, 'Well, this is my GOLD,' showing him my picture that I had drawn a couple of months before. 'This has my goals on it, my opportunities, my love and my dreams.'

The picture portrayed me as an international speaker (with head mic) standing on a massive stage that was held up by my golden gang, who were standing on top of the world. The small detail showed that I was wearing a Scout necker, reflecting the voluntary work I do and the potential legacy of a goal-setting programme and badge achievement award system that I'd love to run within Scouting, even with my very own badge. A pile of books that I had written were on the stage with me and I even had a samurai sword in my belt, representing my desire to share my story on a speaking tour of Japan. The sword would be a gift and 'don't lean on your excuses' would be engraved on the blade in Japanese script. A network of computers represented my 'Good to GOLD' workshop being available online for the whole world to access. I'd also drawn some houses to represent an established property portfolio and some stocks and shares that were moving in the right direction. There was a big family house where we were all living together with an array of cars parked outside and a helicopter on the helicopter pad – you know, for when it was needed.

'Wow,' said Rob. 'This is amazing and I love the detail and the vision that you've put into this – but where is your five-year plan?'

'Oh,' I said as I shared my podium project plan and a few SMARTIE goals that I'd produced.

'Hmm,' said Rob. 'And do you have anything else, something that ties this all together in a structured, time-based way?'

'Oh, this is it; this is all I have,' I admitted.

Now, the thought of sitting down and filling in a big spreadsheet with facts and figures and formulating a structured five-year plan bores the hell out of me whereas drawing a picture and filling in building blocks is a lot more fun. However, Rob had an idea.

'We're going to create a vision orbit,' said Rob.

'Wow, that sounds great. What is it?' I enquired.

Creating a vision orbit

Year by year

A vision orbit is drawn on a big sheet of paper and looks like a dart board where present day is in the middle at the bullseye and the far outer ring is the fifth year. From the outside coming inwards you have another ring that represents the fourth year then another for the third year, second, and first year and then you're back at the bullseye, the centre of the circle.

The orbit is split into quadrants and each one of those related to a part of my drawing or part of my GOLD. So, for example, if I wanted to have written three books by my fifth year, I had to ask myself how many I would have to have written by my fourth year or third, second or first and then I'd write that down on the vision orbit. My desired turnover in five years' time would be written on the outer ring and then I'd estimate what my turnover would realistically be in the preceding years down to the end of my first year.

For each of my goals I could break it up year by year bringing it back to the first year. Creating this was enjoyable as I was still using my drawing as a starting block for the fifth year on each quadrant and then using the blocks from my podium project plan as guidance. By the end of the exercise, I could see what I had to do by the end of my first year to be on track to achieve my GOLD by the fifth year. I even had to get a calculator out for some of the sections just to ensure that all the figures married up and balanced out. This was serious stuff. 'How many speaking gigs and workshops will I have to have completed and how many books will I have to have sold to achieve the expected turnover in year three?'

As my vision orbit developed it transformed my drawing and podium project plan into goals with realistic values and stable time elements. I could see that some goals could potentially be achieved sooner than anticipated although some would be later, but either way they were still there. Keeping the dream alive.

Exercise 10: your golden vision orbit

Now it's your turn. It's time to start planning, including some long-term deadlines, by creating your own vision orbit. The exercise here is more of a reference as I'd suggest that you have one produced on a big sheet of paper to enable you to write all the detail on it.

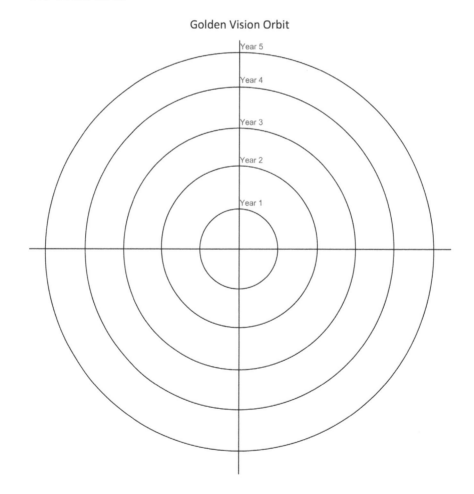

Golden Vision Orbit

Month by month

Now that I had my overall vision orbit I could start breaking down the year goals into more realistic and achievable chunks. Rob encouraged me to choose which goals I was going to work on first. That's a tough decision as I worked out that I had 26 goals I wanted to work on. I viewed my golden vision orbit and trusted my gut as I scanned the sheet. Deep down, my subconscious knew which goals I should be concentrating on – the ones that would propel me closer to my GOLD, the ones I was passionate about and sometimes the ones that I didn't really want to focus on but knew I had to.

The second thing Rob asked me to do was to write them on to the wall chart that he supplied. It was set out as groups of three months with 12-week blocks. Using the SMARTIE goal sheets that I mentioned in Chapter 5, I worked out what exactly I wanted to achieve in the three-month segment for each of the goals, making sure that these three-month goals became specific, measurable, achievable, results driven and with a timescale allocated to them. The completion of these goals would ultimately lead me to my GOLD, so to me they were inspiring and connected to my golden soul. They were also emotional. The goal descriptions were applied to the planner, which left 12-week blocks that needed filling in with a task that would lead me through the months. I used my podium project plan method to work out the tasks I needed to complete and then I was ready to apply them to the chart.

Exercise 11: your month-by-month chart

The month-by-month chart is overleaf; however, for you to fully complete it with the necessary details, it really needs to be on a big sheet like a wall chart.

Your Golden Hour - Month by Month

Goal	Week 1	Week 2	Week 3	Week 4	Week 5	Week 6	Week 7	Week 8	Week 9	Week 10	Week 11	Week 12	Week 13
	Date:	Date:	Date:	Date:	Date:	Date:	Date:	Date:	Date:	Date:	Date:	Date:	Date:
Goal:													
1													
2													
3													
Goal:													
1													
2													
3													
Goal:													
1													
2													
3													
Goal:													
1													
2													
3													

Week by week

For this part I used some sticky notes, writing the task on the note before sticking it on the chart. I then inserted them onto the wall chart one after the other in the sequence in which they needed completing. Some tasks were going to take longer than one week but that was fine as I just extended the task onto a couple of notes. The sticky notes work well as I can move them to the left when I'm ahead of myself or to the right in unexpectedly challenging times. Life can get complicated so it's good to have a bit of flexibility. I just have to make sure it doesn't become a habit. 'It's just a blip,' I affirm to myself. 'Let's get back on track.' There, in front of me, was a plan that showed me what I had to do week by week that would take me to my three-monthly goal and onwards to my yearly goal.

Day by day

Splitting my SMARTIE goal week by week is great and prepares me for the next stage, day by day. Using my weekly planning sheet, I note down my overall goals for the week ahead and then what day I will work towards them in order to complete them by the end of the week. Committing a dedicated time slot to the action that I'm taking is key to its completion even if it's just one hour and especially if it's a golden hour. (I'll cover this in more detail soon.)

Exercise 12: your weekly and daily lists

The day-by-day worksheet is below for reference for the weeks ahead as you plan for the completion of your goals.

<u>Week Commencing Date:</u>

Week and Day
To-do List

Goals for the Week	Goals for the Week
1	5
2	6
3	7
4	8

Monday

Thursday

Tuesday

Friday

Wednesday

Saturday

Sunday

Comments:

> **GOLDEN NUGGET**
> *'A commitment to a moment in time in order to take action is key to the completion of any goal.'*
> – Steve Judge

Important daily routines

In addition to my daily plans, I have a couple of daily habits and routines that help me to manage my time, feel rested and reflect on my day. Here are two of them, one for the end of the day and one as the new day begins.

Golden sunset

I've discovered that sleep is almost a superpower that many of us abuse, and for me to get up consistently at 5.30 am one thing I need to do is to be asleep by 10.30 pm. The first column on my golden sunset routine sheet records the time I'm in bed in order to have a visual record. I then write down three things that I will achieve the next day, which clears my head, or else I'd have a million dreams keeping me awake. I always celebrate my wins, so I write down three things in the day that went well for me. Next comes gratitude and remembering and accepting the things I all too often take for granted: a roof over my head, food in the fridge, family and friends. I love our family roasts on a Sunday. Then I do a little light reading, which is not usually a personal development book but maybe some poetry or fiction. I have a simple meditation technique which by this time may just be a deep breath in, counting 5... 4... 3... 2...1 (and hold) and then breathing out 1... 2... 3... 4... 5. I repeat this three times and then I'm done and ready to sleep. I'm conscious that I should do more on the meditation part as I know the benefits and there are various simple techniques that I could use. Something for me to work on, I guess.

Exercise 13: your golden sunset routine

Here is a copy of the template. Do it for one week and see how it goes.

Monday date: _____   Golden Sunset Routine

Day	Time	Goals for the next day	Congratulations for today	Gratitude 3 things I'm thankful for	Light reading At least one page	Meditation Breathing / Guided meditation (Headspace or Spotify)	z z z Hours asleep	Comments or score out of 10 as to how you feel
M							z z z	
T							z z z	
W							z z z	
T							z z z	
F							z z z	
S							z z z	
S							z z z	

The justified and ancient practice of Wu-Gu

The golden sunset routine supports me in having a great night's sleep so that when my alarm goes off in the morning I can practice Wu-Gu. Let me explain to you what Wu-Gu is. In short, Wu-Gu is an ancient Japanese art that has been passed down from generation to generation. It ensures that the mythical powers and energy that flow through this ancient concept are followed, encompassed and practised in the rising sun of the early morning.

I'm only joking! Wu-Gu simply stands for 'wake up – get up' and I made it up myself. It's simply the practice of not hitting the snooze button, not snuggling down for an extra five minutes, and not ignoring the alarm altogether. When I wake up, I get up. If anything, when I hear my alarm, I'm ready, just like I was when I was an elite athlete getting up for my early morning swim sessions. I wake up and I'm ready to seize the day. I'm empowered to complete my golden morning routine and start on my tasks that I know will take me ever closer to achieving my GOLD.

The golden hour

This chapter started with the harsh explanation of the golden hour being the period of time that can give life or take it away. I'm now using this term to ensure that I make time to take action towards the things in my life that I truly want, my goal, my opportunity, my love and my dream. In this one hour I wholeheartedly and committedly work towards reaching my chosen goal. This time period is called My 'goal-done hour' (do you see what I did there?).

> **GOLDEN NUGGET**
> *'Work expands so as to fill the time available for its completion'*
> – popularly known as Parkinson's Law, C. Northcote Parkinson

I have a one-hour egg timer on my desk (it's gold, of course) and I wind it up and then I'm off. For that one hour of committed time I am fully dedicated to taking action towards achieving my goal. Where possible I turn off my phone and my email and any other applications or distractions that may interrupt me physically or my train of thought. Once I get going, I submerge myself into the depths of what needs doing and time flies by. Strangely, the ticking of the clock reminds me that every second counts and keeps my momentum up as the relaxing non-lyrical music that I play zones me out into a plateaued state of confidence and assertiveness. My goal-done hour is when I aim to complete the task that I have set myself within that deadline and, more than often, I achieve what I set out to do. I'm taking control and giving myself an hour to get done what's important to me. And after a wellness break and maybe some fresh air, I may go for another couple of sessions. My goal-done hour gives me fresh meaning and a new purpose. I use this period of time to move upwards, bettering my life and preventing myself flatlining through it, both personally and professionally.

> **GOLDEN NUGGET**
> *'People often set unrealistic short-term goals in an attempt to achieve more realistic future goals.'*
> – Rob Pickering

The methods that I use by year, month, week, day and hour help me to achieve. Whether you are an entrepreneur, work in a team or even for a whole organisation, the system works. The process of setting specific deadlines and working towards them is the key to success and achievement. But as my business coach Rob recommends, it's best to start on your long-term goals and work backwards. Open up and express your dreams about your specific long-term goals within your organisation or your vision of the business or department in the future. This to me is your GOLD.

Working towards team GOLD

Finding, creating and drawing your GOLD enables you to share the picture with your team or employees. Use the golden vision in combination with your golden vision orbit so that your staff fully understand the journey that everybody is about to embark on. Explain through the golden soul why this journey needs to happen, why it's so important and what the outcome will bring.

The golden gear podium project plan is there to express what needs to be done as well as asking the question, 'What more can be done?'

Use all the members of your golden gang to expand and share the knowledge of one another in order to work towards your GOLD. With everybody on board, the golden vision orbit can be broken down month by month and week by week using the sticky notes system on the wall chart. Everybody can be involved in setting specific and realistic goals using the SMARTIE goal worksheets as well as being proactive about possible barriers that may cause problems on the journey.

Each individual's week ahead can be structured by using the day-by-day worksheets so that everyone will be able to review and set daily tasks and targets that will edge you and your team closer to your goal each and every day. Finally, with the focus-driven activity of the goal-done hour you, your team, department and organisation as a whole will, step by step, complete the journey and achieve your GOLD.

GOLDEN NUGGET
'If time is the thing that's stopping you from accomplishing your dream, then it sounds like you need to get on with it, now.'
– Steve Judge

Now it's your time to shine

If you've followed the exercises in this book, you'll have set your golden map and know where you are and also where you want to be. Drawing your golden vision has enabled you to see what the GOLD in your life is and the golden soul exercise will have helped you realise why it's so important to you.

Your golden gear has given you awareness of how you are

actively going to achieve it, step by step, block by block. Having your golden gang helping you on your journey will enable you to hit those targets and deadlines by using the golden hour concept.

Your future is in your hands and if you're absolutely committed to taking the necessary action towards achievement, then I have one question for you.

Exercise 14: your golden key action list

What immediate action are you willing to take in order to move things forward, right now?

This is your golden key moment. Write down and commit to at least three actions that will unlock the power of your potential for you to achieve the GOLD in your life.

Write your action list here:

Golden key action list

	Action	Date
1.	_____	_____
2.	_____	_____
3.	_____	_____

Why not go further and get some accountability by taking a photo of your actions and sharing them on social media? You can use the hashtag #goodtogold. Feel free to tag me on Instagram at @stevejudgegold. You can also join like-minded people at the Facebook group 'The Golden Touch' or maybe send a personal email to me and tell me about the commitment that you're making: i.Nspire@steve-judge.co.uk

To take dynamic action and be the change that you see in yourself, you either need inspiration, motivation or desperation. In my journey from wheelchair to world champion and beyond, I had all three. Throughout this book I've explained how they have helped me and continue to do so. Now it's over to you.

The most extraordinary life is waiting for you. Take it, it's yours.

Resources

Links to all the exercises and downloadable sheets can be obtained by going to the following URL: steve-judge.co.uk/good-to-gold-resources-page

References

Ashken, S (2016) 'What is Computer Vision? Part 1: Human Vision'. Blippar. URL: blippar.com/blog/2016/06/14/what-computer-vision-part-1-human-vision

Clear, J (2018) *Atomic Habits*. Penguin.

Doran, G T (1981) 'There's a S.M.A.R.T. way to write management's goals and objectives'. *Management Review* November. URL: scribd.com/document/458234239/There-s-a-S-M-A-R-T-way-to-write-management-s-goals-and-objectives-George-T-Doran-Management-Review-1981-pdf

Elrod, H (2012) *The Miracle Morning*. John Murray.

Garton, E & Mankins, M (2015) 'Engaging your employees is good, but don't stop there'. *Harvard Business Review* 9 December. URL: hbr.org/2015/12/engaging-your-employees-is-good-but-dont-stop-there

Judge, S (2019) *Don't Lean On Your Excuses*. Librotas.

Abhilash, K P & Sivanandan, A (2020) 'Early management of trauma: The golden hour'. *Current Medical Issues* 18(1). URL: cmijournal.org/text.asp?2020/18/1/36/277530

Lewis, M (2012) 'Obama's Way'. *Vanity Fair* 11 September. URL: vanityfair.com/news/2012/10/michael-lewis-profile-barack-obama

Science Direct (2022) 'Reticular Activating System'. URL: sciencedirect.com/topics/veterinary-science-and-veterinary-medicine/reticular-activating-system

Sinek, S (2009) *Start with Why: How great leaders inspire everyone to take action*. Penguin.

Recommended reading

Collinson, C (2017) *Improve Your Life*. FCM Publishing.
Cope, A & Whittaker, A (2012) *The Art of Being Brilliant*. Capstone.
Duckworth, A (2017) *Grit*. Vermilion.
Hunt-Davis, B (2011) *Will it Make The Boat Go Faster?* Matador.
McGee, P (2011) *S.U.M.O. (Shut up, Move on)*. Capstone.
Stevenson, S (2016) *Sleep Smarter*. Hay House.
Tracy, B (2011) *No Excuses*. Da Capo Press.

Setting your golden map

Achiever assessments
This link will take you to the online assessments where you can complete the comprehensive focus and achiever exercises. You will then receive a score and a detailed response.
steve-judge.co.uk/good-to-gold-assessments

My golden vision
This link will take you to my current vision as well as the pictures from my past of things that I have achieved.
steve-judge.co.uk/my-golden-vision

My golden music
This link will take you to my music page, where you will be able to view the music that I listen to as well as my playlists – some to keep me motivated and some to take me through the 'wave of resilience'. Don't judge me on my choices – judge me on my methods.
steve-judge.co.uk/steves-golden-music-page

My golden gang

Members of my golden gang that have been specifically mentioned in this book. All members are listed here: steve-judge. co.uk/my-golden-gang

PSA (Professional Speaking Association)

The organisation is for anyone involved in the world of professional speaking. Whether you get paid to speak at conferences, run workshops or are employed by a company and presenting is a significant part of your job then you should check out the PSA here: thepsa.co.uk

Rob Pickering – award-winning business coach: reading. actioncoach.co.uk

Harry Purewal – personal branding and image consultant: agirlnamedharry.com

Natalie Rowe – graphic designer: goshgolly.co.uk

Jo Goodfellow – supportive partner and transformation coach: jogoodfellow.com

Jason Mirpuri – leading bespoke tailor in Hong Kong: lordscustomtailors.com

Penny Haslam (mastermind group) – award-winning speaker, author, coach and trainer: pennyhaslam.co.uk

Liz Hardwick (mastermind group) – digital productivity specialist, professional speaker, digital and online training: DigiEnable. co.uk

Heather Wright (mastermind group) – award-winning speaker, author, coach and trainer: advance-performance.co.uk

Kate Trafford (mastermind group) – Master Coach, author, TEDx speaker: katetrafford.com

James Perryman (mastermind group) – leadership coach, trainer and consultant: momentus.uk.com

Cliff Hewson – website technician: ohsocreative.co.uk

Jayne Petherbridge – hairdresser: esquirebarbering.com

Social media

I'd love to connect with you via social media on any of the following platforms:

Twitter: @stevejudge
LinkedIn: Steve Judge
Facebook: Steven Judge – GOLD
Instagram: @stevejudgegold
YouTube: @SteveJudgeGOLD

Acknowledgements

This book is not for me; it's to help people, inspire others and motivate many. However, I could not have written it unless I had been helped, inspired and motivated along the way. The acknowledgements and thanks for this book go far and wide, from the specific individuals who have shared their wisdom and mentorship to the various subconscious inputs from other sources. I've never considered myself to be a trailblazer but, when you get that burning sensation inside you, a spark of inspiration and a glowing fire of ideas that you need to share, then it comes down to taking action and making things happen. The stories, tools and exercises have always been there from my journey, and the idea of writing this book has been bubbling away for some time, which was frustrating for me due to my impatience. I realise and accept that without that time, I wouldn't have met the people who have helped and inspired me to make this book as good as it is today.

Thank you to my loving and supportive partner Jo, who simply suggested that I start typing the new book and see where it goes. She then had to listen to my ongoing conversations about the book along with the highs, the lows and frustrations as it progressed. Thank you for listening to me as I once again talked about 'my book'. You did so because you understood how important it was to me, which I appreciated and which is one of many reasons why I love you.

Thank you to my amazing business coach Rob Pickering, who fed me with his wisdom, knowledge and expertise. He encouraged and guided me to make that commitment, grab the opportunity and start the process of making this book really happen by introducing structure and accountability.

As you read the book you can't help but appreciate the input that Rob has had from beginning to end – igniting the initial fire within me by using the quote 'Hell on earth is...', and then following this up with support on each of the chapters and most prominently with the tools and advice within the final chapter.

Thank you to my mastermind group where ideas from discussions, mixed with creativity and positive energy, have helped the birth of certain concepts throughout the book. Then, with encouragement and support from the individuals, those ideas have evolved into a clear, understandable and manageable strategy. Collaboration is key when we're seeking out more knowledge than we know ourselves.

Thank you to my book publishing team who have guided me through this book publishing journey. For me, it's very much about knowing what my skills are and knowing my limits, which consequently leads me to also knowing when to ask for help. Thank you to Sue Richardson, Jane Simmonds, Paul East and the rest of the golden gang at The Right Book Company who have made this book pure gold.

The rest of the book, including quotes, connections and theories have come from a multiple of sources. The amazing speakers and facilitators of the Professional Speaking Association. Books, blogs and newsletters that I have read along with webinars and videos that I have watched. Podcasts that I have spoken on and episodes that I have listened to. Films, theatre productions and even television shows have all had an input on my approach to this book. Although I acknowledge and appreciate all of them there are simply too many to list.

Finally, I'd like to thank myself – Steve. Thank you for your drive and dedication to get this book out there. Setting your alarm early in the morning to work on your book before the sun rose showed your grit and determination. Typing away in your office while you could see the tempting blue sky out of the window proved your commitment to your overall GOLD to share your tools in order to empower others to fulfil their dreams. Thank you – just don't forget the celebration and the neck and shoulder massage you promised yourself.

Bring Steve to your organisation

Scout (noun): *A person sent out ahead of a team for reconnaissance to gather information and report back in order to achieve safe passage in reaching their destination.*

Now that you've read this book and participated in the tasks, you have the golden compass in your hand and you'll be well on your way in journeying towards achieving your GOLD, it's time to bring the rest of your team with you. This may be your employees, your department or even your golden gang. Your call to action is to take on the responsibility, the challenge and the honour of leading your team forward on this journey of discovery and achievement. Just like Amelia Earhart or Captain James Cook, you too can lead an expedition in order to gain fulfilment for yourself and your followers.

Steve speaks at team events and conferences and conducts seminars and masterclasses.

He tailors his message to your requirements and is often asked to speak about taking teams from good to GOLD, resilience and motivation.

Speaking
You can book Steve to deliver his award-winning keynote inside your organisation for an upcoming conference or event.

Workshop
Steve can also run the full Good to GOLD workshop for your organisation at a suitable time and location of your choice.

Elearning workshop
This book complements Steve's Good to GOLD elearning workshop, which is available from his website. Multiple sign-up packages are available where all the chapters of this book are covered with the associated exercises as well as a video.

One to one
Steve is happy to have a chat with anyone wanting to move forward on their journey through support, coaching or mentoring. Just give him a shout.

Personalised book purchases
If you wish to purchase more copies of the book for your team, Steve is more than happy to sign each book before dispatch if you order from his website.

For more details about the Good to GOLD programme or any more of Steve's services there are a number of ways to contact him:

Website: steve-judge.co.uk
Email: i.Nspire@steve-judge.co.uk

If you prefer you can call the offices on 07939 220784. We look forward to hearing from you.